PROPERTY LAWS OF THE STATE OF OHIO AFFECTING THE CHURCH

CANON LAW STUDIES
THE CATHOLIC UNIVERSITY OF AMERICA
No. 367

PROPERTY LAWS OF THE STATE OF OHIO AFFECTING THE CHURCH

A DISSERTATION

Submitted to the Faculty of the School of Canon Law of the Catholic University of America in Partial Fulfillment of the Requirements for the Degree of Doctor of Canon Law

by

REVEREND URBAN C. WIGGINS, A.B., J.C.L.
Priest of the Diocese of Columbus

THE CATHOLIC UNIVERSITY OF AMERICA PRESS
WASHINGTON, D. C.
1956

NIHIL OBSTAT:

THOMAS O. MARTIN, Ph.D., S.T.D., J.C.D.
Censor Deputatus

Washingtonii, D.C., 5 junii, 1956.

IMPRIMATUR:

✠ MICHAEL J. READY, D.D.
Episcopus Columbensis

Columbi, die 26 junii, 1956.

Printed by The Abbey Press, St. Meinrad, Indiana

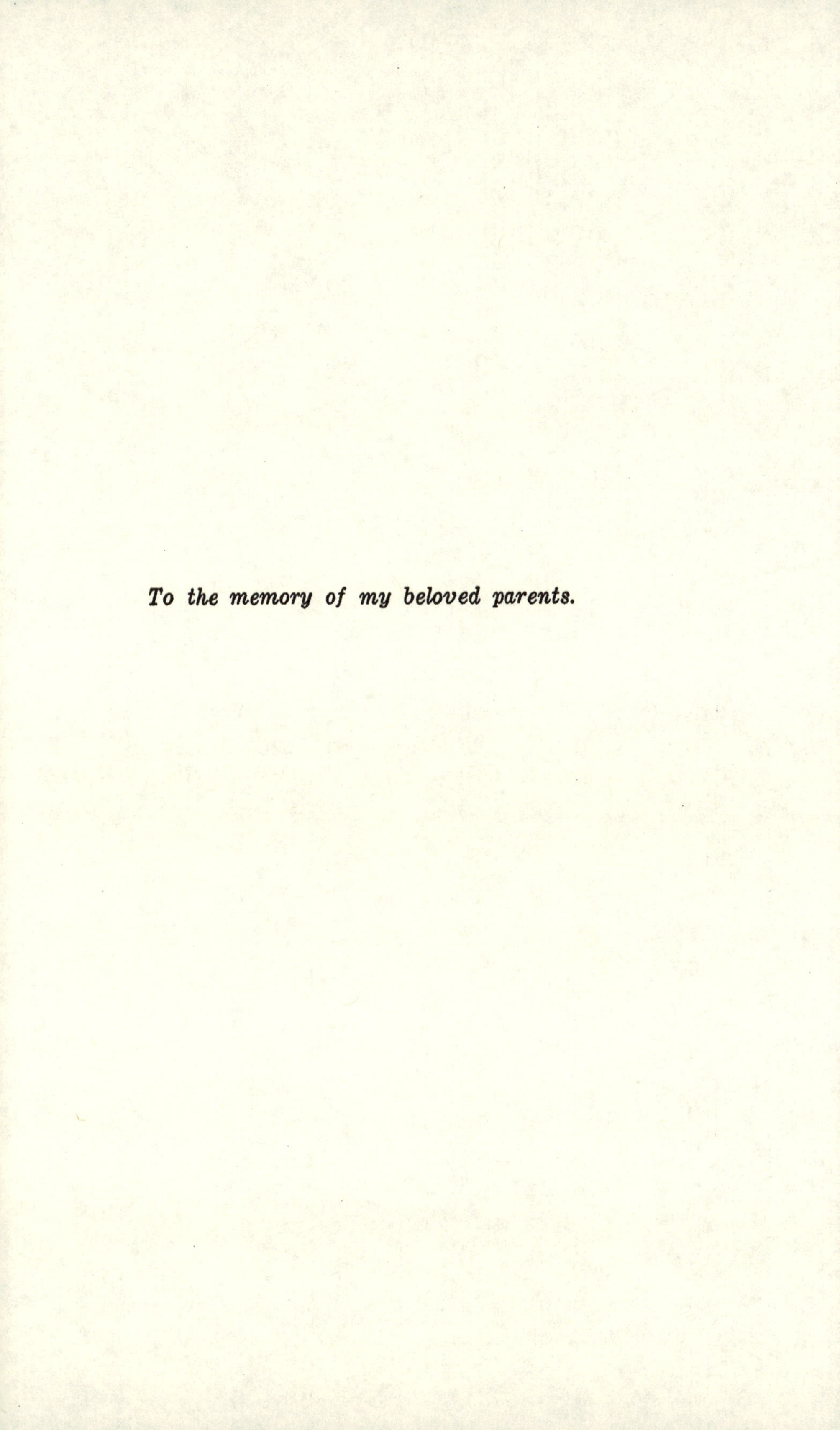

To the memory of my beloved parents.

TABLE OF CONTENTS

Part I
HISTORICAL SYNOPSIS

Part II
PROPERTY LEGISLATION IN CANON LAW AND THE CIVIL LAW OF OHIO

FOREWORD

From the very first days of its appearance upon earth the Catholic Church has announced itself as a visible society pursuing an invisible, spiritual and supernatural end. It has not classified itself on the same footing as any corporation in common law. For more than nineteen centuries the Church has assumed the position of a juridically perfect society, existing in its own right with its own independent sphere of activity, and possessing within itself all of the means necessary to attain its end. In keeping with this position the Church has asserted and constantly insisted upon its complete autonomy as a sovereignty distinct from the State. In word and action it has presented itself as a ruling power comprising all three of the essential functions, legislative, judicial and executive.

This claim to authority over earthly subjects, on the part of the Church, has been challenged by the secular power time and again. The State has not hesitated to question or to deny the Church's right to the exercise of such authority, and this has given rise to one storm after another as the rivalries have continued down through the centuries. Although the Church has always stated emphatically that its mission and activity are primarily of a spiritual nature, it has declared also that it possesses an inherent right to the temporalities which are necessary for the certain and successful achievement of its spiritual purpose. The reason for this claim is founded in the fact that the Church must make use of both material and spiritual elements. The members of the spiritual society are visible members, for they have bodies as well as souls. As subjects of the Church, therefore, they must be governed by both material and spiritual means. The society of the State, however, has not always been ready and willing to accept this fact, for many times it has laid claim to supreme authority in all matters affecting the welfare of its subjects. It has not been wholly receptive to the notion of two supreme societies, existing side by side, free and independent of each other, each exercising its sovereign authority over the same subjects in its own particular domain, spiritual or temporal. Indeed, throughout their long history the conflicts between the two powers have been the result of their grave concern about one or the other expanding itself beyond its due limits.

In developing their systems of law the Church and the State have manifested this concern for protecting themselves against unjust encroachments upon their rights. Every age of their existence together has seen each society formulating laws and assuming attitudes in its relationships with the other. In so doing, the two powers have made efforts either to recognize each other, and thus to exist and function in harmony, or to take a determined stand against each other, and thus to clash on matters of principle in their practical application.

The first part of this dissertation will present a historical synopsis of some of the legal aspects of the relations between the two sovereignties in property matters, and it will examine some of the legislation enacted by both Church and State to declare and vindicate their rights over the acquisition and administration of property. The primary purpose of this study, however, is to make a comparison of the canon law and the civil law of the State of Ohio regarding the acquisition, tenure, and administration of church property, in an effort to determine how and to what extent these two systems are parallel in their legislation, and to what degree the Church is affected in those instances where this parallel does not exist. This work is not intended to give a detailed commentary on all the property laws which are in force in the two systems of law. Such a task would obviously be beyond the scope of one dissertation. It is rather intended here to examine those property laws which chiefly affect the Church in the exercise of its divinely granted rights concerning temporal goods.

The writer is deeply grateful to His Excellency, the

Most Reverend Michael J. Ready, D.D., Bishop of Columbus, Ohio, for the opportunity to undertake graduate studies in Canon Law, and to the members of the Faculty of the School of Canon Law of the Catholic University of America for their kind assistance during the course of these studies and in the preparation of this work.

Part I

HISTORICAL SYNOPSIS

CHAPTER I

THE CLAIM OF THE CHURCH TO TEMPORAL POSSESSIONS IN THE FIRST CENTURIES

ARTICLE I. THE ATTITUDE OF THE STATE TOWARD THE CHURCH'S APPEARANCE AND CLAIM TO AUTHORITY

The presence of so great a number of ambassadors to the Holy See, in the middle of this twentieth century, is a fact most significant and worthy of careful consideration. Although such representatives have not been appointed by all of the temporal powers throughout the world, nevertheless they are in sufficient number to indicate how widely the sovereignty of the Catholic Church, in its own sphere, is recognized and respected by the sovereignty of the State.

In the days of primitive Christianity, however, when the Church was first making its appearance among men, its claim to supreme authority in religious matters came as a shocking announcement. The historian, Joseph Lecler, declared that such a claim was regarded as a scandal and an unheard-of and threatening novelty.[1] Nothing could have been more contrary to the ideas which were prevalent through the whole ancient world than the disassociation of the temporal from the spiritual, of the State from religion.[2]

In the days before Christianity the world knew of one sovereignty only, that of the State, which exercised its sway over both religious and civil life. With the advent of Christianity this unity was destroyed, and there existed, side by side, two distinct sovereignties, each supreme in its particular sphere of activity. Lecler spoke of this dual sovereignty in the following manner:

> The introduction of a dualism of this kind be-

[1] *The Two Sovereignties—A Study of the Relationship Between Church and State* (New York: Philosophical Library, 1952), p. 3 (hereafter cited as *The Two Sovereignties*).

[2] *Ibid.*, Foreword, p. VIII.

> tween religious society and civil society represented in the ancient world a revolution without precedent. The incorporation of Religion in the State was in the cities of antiquity so incontestable a fact that it is useless to insist at any length upon it. Cicero put the whole matter in a nutshell when he wrote: "*Sua cuique civitati religio est, nostra nobis.*" In the Roman Empire, in particular, no self-governing religious body was allowed to exist over against the State. The priests of the official religion were merely State functionaries entrusted with the performance of acts of worship; they were in no sense considered to be the custodians of doctrine; they were not even the people whom it was usual to consult in regard to religious questions. Moreover, the worship of the gods of Rome was a part of one's civic duty; it was required of all loyal subjects. Conquered peoples were indeed allowed to retain their national deities, and the diffusion throughout the Empire of certain cults of Oriental origin was permitted—but on one condition—those who embraced these foreign religions must retain their loyalty to the official gods. Thus while syncretism was allowed in religious matters, exclusiveness was forbidden.[3]

Lecler thus spoke of the Church's appearance and claims as a true Christian revolution in the matter of sovereignty. It was not to be expected, therefore, that the secular power would react toward the Church in any other manner than by strong and determined opposition, for here was an attack upon an ancient and time-honored legal system. It was a matter of established law that religion was a mere creature of the State. Consequently, whoever chose to accept a new religious authority independent of the State obviously was considered to be violating the law. It was a civic duty of all loyal subjects to worship the gods of Rome; indeed, the adoration of the Emperor himself became a legal obligation in the second century. Those who refused to render this worship could only be branded as criminals before the law. Inasmuch as one of the essential

[3] *Ibid.*, p. 8.

functions of government was to punish offenders in proportion to the seriousness of their crimes, the State did not hesitate to employ its coercive power over those who called themselves Christians. Since the alleged crime of the Christians was considered a most serious one of treason, the defensive reaction on the part of the State was most severe. It found its expression in the bloody persecutions during the first centuries of the Christian Era. In regard to these persecutions, Lecler stated:

> . . . The fact that the Christians were thrown to the lions and hunted to death in a thousand different ways is not to be explained merely by the absurd fables which the pagans spread abroad at their expense. It is not to be explained merely by their monotheism or by their scorn of Caesar-worship, for the Jewish nation, which also rejected with horror this supreme form of idolatry, received tolerant treatment. The explanation lies rather in pagan recognition of the fact that, behind Christian universality, lay the complete and absolute negation of the State's claim to sovereignty in religious matters. As a matter of policy, the Emperors could allow a conquered nation, still shuddering from the blows it had received, to maintain with jealous care the exclusive cult of Yahweh. They felt bound, however, to proscribe a new sect which, after detaching itself from all national ties, had constituted itself into a spiritual city and was now calling into question an essential element of sovereignty. It was in vain that the defenders of the Christians praised their pacific spirit, their readiness to be taxed, their devotion to the Empire; their enemies merely replied by asking what was the use of all this parade of loyalty if the Christians claimed the right, in their capacity as a spiritual and universal society, to cut adrift from the State and the national deities? We do not of course deny for a moment either the injustice or the brutality of the persecutions, but it is easy to picture the alarm of the magistrates when faced with a growing sect which proclaimed itself to be universal like the Empire and which, at the same time, threatened one of the

> pillars of the ancient State: its religious authority.[4]

With this correct understanding of the State's position and its attitude toward the Church, it is easier to understand the difficulties which inevitably arose between the two powers concerning property matters. Under Roman Law both private individuals and corporations had the right of acquiring and possessing property. The Empire, however, took quite a while to recognize the Church as a legal entity; rather, it regarded the Church as a private religious group and therefore incapable of the right of acquiring and possessing temporal goods. Because of this lack of recognition a great and important part of the Church's struggle was concerned with the task of providing itself with one of the essential means necessary to carry out its divinely established purpose. It was to be a universal society comprising many officials, departments, and a wide variety of functions. Thus the right to acquire and administer property was imperative for its very maintenance and existence. This was one of the rights which the Church would have to express firmly, and defend and protect most carefully.

Article II. The Practice of the Church in Acquiring and Possessing Property

In view of the rigid attitude of the State toward the Church's claims at the beginning of the Christian Era, the acquisition and possession of property became a matter of grave concern to the Church. It has already been mentioned that the juridical personality of the Church was not formally recognized by the Empire, and therefore its right to acquire temporal goods was not granted at first. To meet this situation in a prudent manner the Church did not assert its right directly; rather, it used the indirect approach. Although there is a controversy about the precise manner in which property was held, it appears that

[4] *Ibid.*, pp. 10-11.

ecclesiastical authorities, as individuals, acquired actual ownership of the necessary goods and likewise managed all of the possessions. It was understood by all of the faithful, however, that the property was held by the ecclesiastical society as such. In the Acts of the Apostles Saint Luke stated that the faithful held all things in common, and that the early Christians sold the property which they owned and gave the price of it to the Apostles to carry on the work of the Church.[5] In this way the Church manifested its right to acquire and possess by actually exercising that right.

Gradually, however, the provincial governors saw that it was beyond their power to deny organization to the Church. Eusebius (263-339) declared that the Church owned property, churches and cemeteries, and that certain Roman Emperors accepted this fact of ownership for they restored to the Church the property which had been confiscated.[6] In fact, the first confiscation of church property as such did not take place until Diocletian came into power in the third century. It must be concluded, therefore, that in spite of the severe opposition which the Church met, particularly in the way of persecution, it nevertheless succeeded in exercising its God-given right from the very beginning of its establishment by Christ as a self-sufficient society.

It was by the Edict of Constantine (313) that the Church's juridical personality was legally acknowledged throughout the Empire. By this edict the essential independence of the Church as a spiritual power was accepted, established and taken for granted as a solid and lasting acquisition. In one sense this was a triumph for the Church, but it must not be misunderstood. It did not mean that the acknowledgment of the Church's independent sovereignty was to see the end of the difficulties between the

[5] Acts, II, 44; IV, 34-37; V, 4.

[6] *Historia Ecclesiastica*, Lib. VII, cap. 13—Migne, *Patrologiae Cursus Completus, Series Graeca* (161 vols., Parisiis, 1857-1866), XX, 674; VII, 30—*MPG*; XX, 719.

two powers. On the contrary, the very fact that they were to exist side by side and exercise true authority over the same subjects meant an active relationship between the two. It was in this relationship that the problems concerning property matters arose.

There should be noted here a policy which the Church saw fit to adopt from its earliest days regarding its ownership and management of property. That policy was to keep its temporal goods free from the undue influence of the lay faithful. The Church learned from the beginning that lay administration of ecclesiastical possessions was not an ideal situation, for it led to many abuses on the part of ambitious laymen, thus defeating the Church's holy purpose. Thomassinus (1619-1695) stated that the Apostles took care of dispensing church property and that they were assisted by a group of laymen and holy women, but he added that this arrangement did not continue to prove satisfactory and that eventually the work was done by a group of deacons.[7] It was in view of this policy being attacked and disregarded so often by lay rulers that the Church faced so many of its difficulties in property matters. It must be remembered that the secular authorities were included among the lay faithful, and this necessarily made the task of correcting abuses more difficult. To carry on its work successfully, therefore, the Church found it necessary to keep its temporal possessions immune from all encroachment by lay authorities. This immunity meant the freedom of ecclesiastical possessions from all tributes or payment of taxes which were imposed upon temporal goods by the civil law.[8] To achieve such immunity the Church dealt with abuses by carefully drawn legislation. In some cases laymen were permitted to function as administrators, either in an authoritative capacity with power to act, or as

[7] *Vetus et Nova Ecclesiae Disciplina circa Beneficia et Beneficiarios*, 10 vols., pars III, lib. I, cap. 1 (hereafter cited as *Vetus et Nova Ecclesiae Disciplina*).

[8] Wernz, Ius Decretalium (6 vols., Romae, 1898-1914), Vol. III, tit. V, n. 146 (hereafter cited as Wernz).

consultors only. The early councils, however, repeatedly condemned all lay usurpation of power,[9] and it must be admitted that their efforts met with some degree of success. Constantine the Great (306-337) was very liberal in exempting the Catholic churches from the payment of taxes, and with the exception of Julian the Apostate the other Roman Emperors allowed exemptions at least to the extent that the Church was not burdened with extraordinary taxes and heavy responsibilities.[10]

The most flagrant abuses of lay encroachment upon church property took place in the first centuries of the Middle Ages. These centuries witnessed the appearance of the proprietary churches and the feudal system of land tenure. This system was based on the theory that the king owned all of the land of the country in fee. As supreme lord he retained full control over the property and the churches built upon it. According to this system, a church formed the center of a separate property-complex. The altar and the ground on which it stood were considered the principal thing, and all of the rest was merely an adjunct. The church building, its fixtures, vestments and utensils, books and bells, the offerings, first fruits and the dues levied by the priest for his services were all adjuncts. Nothing was delivered over to the control of church authorities at the time of the church's consecration, but everything remained the property of the lay lord or of the Saint to whom it was dedicated, with the lay lord acting as his guardian. The lay lord or proprietor exercised full civil

[9] Council of Ancyra (314), canon 15—Hardouin, *Acta Conciliorum et Epistolae Decretales ac Constitutiones Summorum Pontificum* (12 vols., Parisiis, 1714-1715), I, 327 (hereafter cited as Hardouin); Council of Antioch (341), canon 24—Hardouin, I, 603,606; Council of Vaison (442), canon 4—Hardouin, I, 1788; Council of Arles (443), canon 47—Hardouin, II, 777; Council of Agde (506), canon 6—Hardouin, II, 998; I Council of Orleans (511), canon 5—Hardouin, II, 1009; Council of Clermont-Auvergne (535), canon 5—Hardouin, II, 1181.

[10] Wernz, III, n. 146; Cf. Martin, "*Theodosius' Church Laws*" *The American Ecclesiastical Review*, CXXII (1950), 430.

rights over the church and its possessions except for the stipulation that the church was not to be diverted from its purpose. The lord could therefore sell, exchange, or bestow it freely as a whole, give it as a dowry or otherwise alienate it. He could devise it, grant it as a fief, or lease it; he could also mortgage it. The law gave the manorial lord full direction and control over the church. As a result, a share of church authority passed into the hands of the lord. All churches founded by private persons and all places of worship which fell into the hands of laymen, in virtue of the extensive secularizations of church property, were private churches. The lord appointed and dismissed the priest who administered the church and exercised his office on the lord's behalf.[11]

Such a private church system was beset with obvious dangers. In every proprietary church the episcopal authority over the church and its ministers was radically challenged. This invasion of ecclesiastical administration by laymen of princely status brought with it the added abuses of commendatory abbeys, feudal tithes, lay investiture, and the lesser corruptions of patronage in matters of church property.

The Church constantly made efforts to oppose these abuses by way of rigid legislation. As early as the year 495, Pope Gelasius had denied founders and builders any rights over a church.[12] The Synod of Rome (502) decreed that laymen could not determine anything in the Church, *"cui subsequendi manet necessitas, non auctoritas imperandi."*[13] The Council of Meaux (845) legislated that no power could force one to grant lands or other property *in pre-*

[11] Stutz, "The Proprietary Church as an Element of Mediaeval Germanic Ecclesiastical Law," *Studies in Mediaeval History* (edited by Geoffrey Barroclough, 2 vols., Oxford, 1938), II, 41-47.

[12] C. 26, C. XVI, q. 7—Jaffé, *Regesta Pontificum Romanorum ab condita ecclesia ad annum post Christum natum MCXCVIII* (2 ed., G. Wattenbach, F. Kaltenbrunner, P. Ewald, S. Loewenfeld, 2 vols., Lipsiae, 1885-1888), JK, n. 416 (hereafter cited as JK, JE and JL).

[13] C. 1, D. XCVI—JK, n. 757.

cario, and that he who took property from a moral person within the Church was guilty not only of theft but of sacrilege, and was bound to make restitution.[14] The IV General Council of Constantinople (869-870) distinguished between church property and the property of individual churchmen. It decreed that the former was independent of all lay control and that no secular person could take away property that had been possessed by the Church for a period of thirty years, even though the Church could not show any transfer of title.[15]

Regardless of the Church's opposition to these abuses by lay encroachment, the proprietary church regime won a victory during the Middle Ages, for by the beginning of the eighth century this theory affected the legal system of the entire Western Church, and private or proprietary churches sprang up everywhere, dominated always by lay lords. Although the Church continued to condemn all usurpation of power on the part of the secular authorities and gradually succeeded in obtaining immunity to a great extent, nevertheless it was destined to take a still firmer stand against secular interference with its possessions. This action was started in the legislation adopted by the I General Council of the Lateran (1123) and during the twelfth and thirteenth centuries Church and State engaged in a long series of disputes over property matters. Perhaps the climax of these disputes was the legal action taken by Pope Boniface VIII (1294-1303) against King Philip IV (1285-1314) of France, the background of which calls for a close examination.

Article III. Decrees of the Popes and the General Councils

It was after the beginning of the twelfth century that the Church took its most rigid stand in legislating to put

[14] Canon 22—Mansi, *Sacrorum Conciliorum Nova et Amplissima Collectio* (53 vols. in 60, Parisiis, 1901-1927), XIV, 823 (hereafter cited as Mansi).

[15] Canons 15, 18—Hardouin, V, 905, 907.

an end to the above-mentioned abuses of lay encroachment. By an act of the I General Council of the Lateran (1123) all disposition of ecclesiastical property by laymen was made entirely unlawful. The Council decreed that lay persons, regardless of their piety, had no power to dispose of anything belonging to the Church, but according to the Canons of the Apostles the supervision of all ecclesiastical affairs belonged to the bishop, whose duty it was to administer them in keeping with God's will. It was declared, therefore, that if any prince or other layman should take upon himself the disposition, control or ownership of church goods or property, he was to be judged guilty of sacrilege.[16] In substance this decree was a repetition of similar conciliar and synodal decrees of former centuries, but the I General Council of the Lateran was not a local, but a general council with the weight of supreme church authority. It declared that the Church's property rights belong to it essentially as a juridically perfect society, and not by virtue of a favorable concession of the secular powers. Furthermore, the Council was held at the beginning of the period which saw the Church at the height of its power and prestige. This period continued through the twelfth and thirteenth centuries, reaching its peak during the reign of Pope Innocent III. During these two centuries the Church convoked six ecumenical councils, each of which legislated in a similar manner concerning property affairs. The II General Council of the Lateran (1139) repeated the decree quoted above in much the same manner.[17]

The III General Council of the Lateran (1179) deplored the abuses of the princes in exacting from the clergy excessive grants and subsidies. It declared that, for the future, the properties of the Church could be taxed only if

[16] Canon 4—Mansi, XXI, 282.

[17] Canon 25: "*Si quis praeposituras, praebendas vel alia ecclesiastica beneficia de manu laici acceperit, indigne suscepto careat beneficio. Juxta namque decreta sanctorum patrum, laici, quamvis religiosi sint, nullam tamen habent disponendi de ecclesiasticis facultatibus potestatem.*" Mansi, XXI, 532.

the bishops and clergy recognized or admitted its necessity. Furthermore this Council placed under censure those who presumed to interfere with the Church's property rights.[18]

Under Pope Innocent III the greatest of the General Councils of the Lateran was held in 1215. Known as the IV General Council of the Lateran, it repeated in still stronger language what had been decreed time and time again by preceding councils and synods. It made specific mention of secular princes and forbade them any kind of authoritative control over the administration of church property. It set down a yet stronger safeguard by decreeing that the Pope himself had to be consulted before the clergy were permitted to confer any grant upon lay princes.[19] The I General Council of Lyons (1254) insisted upon church property being safeguarded. It forbade rectors of churches to put themselves or their churches under obligation to others, or to contract debts which would prove a source of trouble at the hands of the lay faithful.[20] The II General Council of Lyons (1274) directed that whoever had, through being the founder or through custom, any right as *advocatus* or any similar rights over churches, monasteries and charitable foundations, was not permitted to abuse them or to claim any of the revenue except during the time of vacancy.[21]

This specific and repeated mention of the secular powers in the Church's legislation during the twelfth and thirteenth centuries indicates how determined was the interference of the State in ecclesiastical affairs, particularly in matters

[18] Canons 14 and 19: "*...Praeterea, quia in tantum quorumdam laicorum processit audacia, ut episcoporum auctoritate neglecta, clericos instituant in ecclesiis, et removeant etiam cum voluerint, possessiones quoque, atque alia bona ecclesiastica, pro sua plerumque voluntate distribuant, et tam ecclesias ipsas quam earum homines, taliis, et exactionibus praesumant gravare; eos qui amodo ista commiserint, anathemate decernimus feriendos...*" Mansi, XXII 225.

[19] C. 4, 7, X, *De immunitate ecclesiarum, cemeteriorum, et rerum ad eas pertinentium,* III, 49; Canon 46—Mansi, XXII, 1030.

[20] Canon 13—Mansi, XXIII, 622.

[21] Canon 12—Mansi, XXIV, 89.

concerning church property. The fact that the Church reached the zenith of its power and prestige at this point of history does not mean that its influence was not under attack by the other sovereignty. On the contrary, since much wealth had passed into the Church's possession during the course of the Middle Ages, the secular princes were quite interested in exercising effective control over such wealth to fill the needs of the kingdom. One knows, from the annotations of the glossators on the *Decretum Gratiani* and the Decretals, that civil rulers issued decrees concerning the disposition of ecclesiastical property. In substance the glossators repeated the principle, *"Laicis etiam religiosis super ecclesiis et personis ecclesiasticis nulla sit attributa facultas."* They declared that the decrees of secular princes had no effect upon the temporal goods of the Church since laymen, including princes, were not invested with powers over such property.[22] They insisted upon the Church's inherent right to acquire and possess property independently of all State authority. They defended all church property as being immune from all control by lay rulers inasmuch as the Church's rights were granted to it not by civil, but by divine authority.[23] The legal action of the State toward ecclesiastical possessions, however, became more and more severe. This is evident from the counteraction of the popes in imposing greater penalties upon transgressors of their decrees. Typical examples of such counteraction are found in the *Liber Sextus* of Boniface VIII. There one finds a decree of Pope Alexander IV (1254-1261) legislating against the actions of certain delegates of the King of France. Those civil officials had been limiting the amount of property which the Church could acquire. They were, moreover, forcing the clergy to alienate ecclesiastical possessions or to sell them or transfer ownership in some other

[22] *Glossa Ordinaria* ad c. 1, D. XCVI, s.v. *Illud autem; Casus* ad c. 1, D. XCVI.

[23] C. 9, X, *de immunitate ecclesiarum*, III, 49; c. 10, X, *de constitutionibus*, I, 2; c. 2, 12, X, *de rebus ecclesiae alienandis vel non*, III, 13.

manner. The Pope, upon learning this, spoke out authoritatively regarding his office as guardian of all the churches. He repeated the principle of the Church's right, as a self-sufficient society, to acquire and possess property. Finally, he outlawed all further abuses under threat of penalties.[24] The tenor of this decree was the most determined of its kind. Alexander IV left no doubt in the minds of all, prince and pauper, that he realized his powerful position and was invoking the fullness of his apostolic authority.

One of the most extreme and historically most publicized instances of a clash between the two sovereignties of Church and State over property matters was in the bitter dispute between Pope Boniface VIII and King Philip the Fair of France. The juridical actions of both powers for two centuries had prepared the way for this argument, and the tension which increased with each dispute over respective rights was most certainly to reach a climax in a bitter struggle for supremacy.

History records many factors which caused or contributed to the trouble between Church and State in the persons of Boniface VIII and Philip the Fair, but the burden of excessive taxation and the unjust procedure by which it was levied against clerics and ecclesiastical possessions was the basis for the property dispute. King Philip of France, like many of his predecessors and contemporaries, was convinced of his right, as a secular monarch, to exercise control over the possessions of his subjects, especially when the urgent need of the kingdom demanded it. In conducting his military campaigns against England and against the Sicilian revolt, Philip was determined to subsidize his armies by means of revenue collected from every possible source. The rich temporalities of the Church were no exception, and the civil rulers made use of extreme measures to exact the fullest possible tax from the clergy.

The Church insisted upon the right of immunity for its

[24] C. 1, *de immunitate ecclesiarum,* III, 23, in VI°.

possessions, but did not hesitate to contribute generously to any national emergency. It usually authorized a tenth of its revenues to be granted to the State. On occasions of extreme emergency a greater amount was freely given. The establishment of the subsidies was determined by the needs of the kings and the zeal of the clergy. The payment of the tithes was at first free and spontaneous. Later it was requested by the kings and authorized by the Pope and the bishops. At times it became an obligation for the clergy to pay on account of the urgent necessity, but their basic right to consent or refuse the tax always remained intact.[25]

By 1296, however, the princes of the various kingdoms were disregarding the Church's claims almost entirely and were demanding the most abundant subsides from the individual churches. So great became the burden of these imposts, and so belligerent were the secular officials in demanding the exactions that the clergy made a special appeal to Pope Boniface VIII for protection against such extortions. The Pope, from his dealings with Philip, was well aware of the abuses. In response to the appeal he first sat in consultation with the Cardinals and then took legal action by promulgating his famous bull, *Clericis laicos*.[26]

The glossator divided this decretal of Boniface VIII into three parts. First there was expressed the *status quaestionis*, in which the Pope explained the fact and seriousness of the burdens imposed by the laity.[27] It must be concluded that the laity mentioned were those invested with authority by the secular powers, for Boniface deplored the fact that so many of the clergy were subjecting themselves to the

[25] Cf. Tosti-Donnelly, *History of Pope Boniface VIII and His Times: With Notes and Documentary Evidence* (six books in one, New York: Christian Press Association, 1911), p. 208 ff. (hereafter cited as Tosti-Donnelly).

[26] Cf. c. 3, *de immunitate ecclesiarum*, III, 23, in VI°.

[27] Glossa Ordinaria, ad c. 3, *de immunitate ecclesiarum*, III, 23, in VI°, s.v. *Clericis, in prima*.

abuses because they feared the civil power more than the Eternal Majesty.[28]

In the second part of the decretal the Pope, by invoking his apostolic authority, began to apply his remedy to correct the abuses.[29] It was the most serious remedy of its kind that had been employed up to that time because of the extent of the excommunications imposed upon clergy and laity alike. Before the *Clericis laicos* lay rulers were forbidden to compel clerics to pay taxes and other exactions, but clerics could freely contribute, in the manner of a gratuitous gift, provided they had the consent of their bishop. If, however, they paid the taxes without the consent, no punishment was imposed upon them. Many clerics therefore, fearing men more than God, made the contributions.[30] In the *Clericis laicos,* however, not only were laymen excommunicated *ipso facto* if they compelled the clergy to pay the taxes, but clerics themselves, if they contributed in the manner of a gratuitous gift without the Pope's authority, were also excommunicated *ipso facto,* and an interdict was imposed upon communities which were at fault in this matter.[31]

The third part of the decretal makes reference to special privileges which had previously been granted to some of the secular princes. Among these privileges was, for example, the promise of never being excommunicated. Pope Boniface clearly stated that all such privileges were revoked if those who enjoyed them violated the provisions of the papal bull. All transgressors without exception, therefore, incurred the censure *ipso facto.*[32]

Two fundamental principles were contained in this legislation of Boniface VIII. The first was that both clergy and

[28] Cf. c. 3, *de immunitate ecclesiarum,* III, 23, in VI°.

[29] *Ibid.,* s.v. *Nos igitur.*

[30] *Glossa Ordinaria,* ad c. 3, *de immunitate ecclesiarum,* III, 23, in VI°, s.v. *Pro Intellectu.*

[31] *Loc. cit.*

[32] Cf. c. 3, de immunitate ecclesiarum, III, 23, in VI°, s.v. *Non obstantibus.*

laity should have equal rights to determine the need and the amount of their subsidies to the crown. The second principle stated that, when there was a question of appropriation of the revenues of the Church for a secular purpose, the clergy should consult the Pope for his decision.

Philip the Fair protested this legislation vigorously because it deprived him of such a great source of wealth. He immediately published an edict affecting ecclesiastical immunities. It forbade under severe penalties the exportation of money. None was to be sent out of the kingdom, not even to the Holy See for pious causes. The constitution decreed that the king could pass laws relating to the good of laymen and clerics alike, over whom, as vassals, he as prince could exercise his power, but tithes, the offerings, and private goods which the faithful had left to the churches for the good of their souls, he could not touch. Philip's edict, therefore, openly violated the canons which forbade laymen to interfere with the administration and spending of the ecclesiastical revenues. As a result, many French beneficiaries residing outside of the kingdom were deprived of their means of support. Among these beneficiaries, of course, was the Pope himself who was accustomed to receive from France offerings of the pious faithful for the recovery of the Holy Land and for the Holy See.

In reply to the royal edict Boniface published the Papal Bull, *Ineffabilis,* in which he assured Philip that he did not forbid the clergy to contribute to the defense and needs of the kingdom, but that they were to do so only with his permission for he wished to put a stop to the extreme burdens of taxation which were being imposed upon the clergy by the royal agents.[33] This explanation, however, was ineffectual with Philip, and he was quick to take advantage of the papal bull. He forced Boniface into retracing his steps, for moved by the dangers which were threatening France the Pope issued the Bull, *Coram illo fatemur,* in which he declared himself ready to offer the goods of the Church for

[33] Cf. Tosti-Donnelly, pp. 167-170.

the conservation of the king and the kingdom. In response to this pronouncement Philip withdrew his edicts with the result that the Pope went a step farther. He published the Bull, *Noveritis nos,* which was a formal and unconditional refutation of the Bull, *Clericis laicos.* It stated that he recognized Philip's right to tax the clergy, in case of necessity, without consent of the Holy See. Finally, he granted Philip one-half of the money destined for the liberation of the Holy Land.[34]

[34] Baronius, *Annales Ecclesiastici* (37 vols., Barri-Ducis, 1864-1883) *ad ann.* 1297, nos. 58, 59.

CHAPTER II

PROPERTY LEGISLATION OF THE CHURCH AND THE STATE IN ENGLAND

ARTICLE I. TAXATION AND ALIENATION

In England, as in France, there arose disputes between Church and State over property matters, especially taxation and alienation of ecclesiastical possessions. The subject of taxation was usually treated under three headings; first, the authority by which the tax was imposed; second, the description of persons on whom, and property on which, it was levied; third, the determination of the amount for which the individual was liable. King Henry I (1100-1135) and his two successors, Henry II (1154-1189) and Richard I (1189-1199), adopted a system of imposing a tax simply by signifying the king's necessities. The king indicated, both to his assembled vassals and to the country at large through the sheriffs, the sums which he wanted and the basis on which he demanded them. It was not until towards the end of the reign of Richard I that there appeared anything like a formal grant or discussion of a grant in the national council. It was then that the idea began to develop that representation should accompany taxation. This was partially due to the constant resistance, on the part of the prelates of England, to the collection of revenues on ecclesiastical property.[1]

It was in the middle of the twelfth century that the two sovereignties came into conflict in the persons of King Henry II and Thomas Becket, Archbishop of Canterbury (1162-1170). The beginning of that long dispute was caused by a determination, on the part of the king, to make a change in the taxation system which would be beneficial to the royal revenues. From the very beginning of his

[1] Stubbs, *The Constitutional History of England* (Oxford: The Clarendon Press, 1891), pp. 618, 620, 622 (hereafter cited as *Constitutional History*).

reign, Henry II brought under contribution the lands held by the churches. Thomas, seeing how the king's plan led to abuses of the Church's immunities, consistently refused to consent to the increased tax. The determination displayed by both king and archbishop eventually resulted in the slaying of Thomas.

It is significant to note that the dispute was the first case of any opposition to the king's will in the matter of taxation recorded in the national history of England.[2] It began a series of difficulties, however, which were to take place through the centuries. After the archbishop rejected the plan of Henry II and refused to accept the customs in use under Henry I, the king ordered them to be reduced to writing after they had first been ascertained by recognition. In 1164 they were formally included in a document which was known as the Constitutions of Clarendon.

The Constitutions were sixteen in number and were described as a part of a great scheme of administrative reform by which the debatable ground between the spiritual and temporal powers could be brought within the reach of common justice. Thomas, however, did not see them in such light. He contended that they were incompatible with the freedom of the clergy.[3] This freedom Henry denied when he imposed his system of taxation upon ecclesiastical possessions. By doing so he was directly violating the solemn decree of the I General Council of the Lateran (1123), which forbade any prince or layman to take upon himself the disposition, control or ownership of church goods or property.[4]

Article II. The Mortmain Statues of the Thirteenth and Fourteenth Centuries

The constant resistance of the Church to the State's demands regarding taxation gradually led to the formula-

[2] *Ibid.*, p. 500.

[3] *Ibid.*, p. 505.

[4] Canon 4—Mansi, XXI, 282.

tion and adoption of the Great Charter, or *Magna Charta,* as it is customarily called. The lay barons recognized the need for such a charter, for the excessive taxation which was imposed to meet King Richard's demands for money had sown the seeds of increased opposition to the king. The growing unpopularity of the government centered around the king himself. It was finally acknowledged that the interests of all classes of people and the need to provide for them had to be given careful consideration.[5]

The *Magna Charta* was first published in the year 1215 during the reign of King John (1199-1216). It was reissued under Henry III (1216-1272) in 1216 and again in 1217, at both times with considerable revision. At the beginnning of the Charter stood the clause which guaranteed the liberty of the Church: *"In primis concessisse Deo et praesenti carta nostra confirmasse, pro nobis et haeredibus nostris in perpetuum quod Anglicana ecclesia libera sit, et habeat iura sua integra, et libertates suas illaesas. . . ."*[6] The freedom which the Charter granted, however, was not granted entirely in property matters. In spite of the Charter's words, and in spite of the solemn decree of the IV General Council of the Lateran (1215), Henry III added a clause which forbade anyone to give his land to any religious house, and thenceforth hold as tenant thereof, without permission of the king. It likewise forbade a religious house to accept the land, and the penalty for a violation was to be a forfeiture of the land to the lord of the fief.[7] This was one of the first English statutes which

[5] Holdsworth, *A History of English Law* (4, ed., 13 vols., London: Methuen & Co., LTD., 1936), II, 207-211 (hereafter cited as Holdsworth).

[6] Stubbs, Select Charters of English Constitutional History (4. ed., London: The Clarendon Press, 1936), pp. 207-211 (hereafter cited as Select Charters).

[7] 9 Henry III, c. 36—"Non licet alicui de cetero dare terram suam alicui domui religiosae, ita quod illam resumat tenendam de eadem domo: nec liceat alicui domui religiosae terram alicuius sic accipere, quod tradat illam ei a quo ipsam recepit tenendam: si quis autem de caetero terram suam domui religiosae sic dederit, et super hoc con-

affected the alienation of property. The alienation was a device by which the donor gave the land to the corporation with the agreement that he was to use it during his lifetime just as if he were the real owner. Upon his death the corporation attained full feudal ownership. The clause in the *Magna Charta* forbade this transfer of temporal goods in favor of the Church. Such a prohibition opposed the rights of the Church over property by restricting its power to acquire and possess. These restrictions were placed upon the Church's rights primarily because the feudal lords, including the crown itself, were not enriched by the revenues from the property as they were when the vassal was a physical person. Juridical persons, like a monastery or a church, when holding land, did not render to the lord the customary services which brought him considerable revenue. Such church corporations, moreover, did not pay the taxes imposed upon physical persons and therefore they came to be known as *manus mortuae.* Every acquisition of property by them was considered a detriment to the secular prince. This prepared the way for the mortmain statues which violated the inherent right of the Church to acquire and possess property. The clause of the *Magna Charta* was enforced by the Provisions of Westminster in 1259. Canon 14 of the Provisions stated: *"Viris autem religiosis non liceat ingredi feodum alicuius sine licentia capitalis domini, de quo scilicet res ipsa immediate tenetur."*[8]

In 1279, the statute, *De Viris Religiosis,* which was called the first statute of mortmain, put a stop to all sales or gifts of land to religious houses without the king's permission. It stated that no person, religious or otherwise, may presume to buy or sell, or under the color of gift or lease, or by reason of any other title whatsoever, to receive of any man, or by any other craft or device to appropriate to

vincatur, donum suum penitus cassetur, ut terra illa domino suo illius feodi incurratur." Evans, *A Collection of Statutes* (London, 1917), p. 343.

[8] Cf. Stubbs, *Select Charters,* p. 404.

himself any lands or tenements under pain of forfeiture of the same whereby such lands or tenements may any wise come into mortmain.[9] The statute, *Quia Emptores*, enacted in 1290, directed that "the sales or purchases of lands or tenements, or any parcels of them, shall in no wise come into mortmain either in part or in whole, neither by policy nor craft, contrary to the form of the statute made thereupon of late."[10] By this statute King Edward I (1272-1307) authorized the alienation of land, but he expressly stated that this should not be understood as authorizing any kind of alienation in mortmain. In a later statute a plan was outlined for such alienation to take place in certain cases, but always with the permission of the king and the intermediate lords.

It was at this time that Pope Boniface VIII published the papal bull, *Clericis laicos*, which has been mentioned above. It came at a time when Edward I was attempting to exact heavy taxes from laity and clergy alike to finance the war with Scotland. Because of the bull, and in keeping with former legislation, the clergy consistently refused to make the contributions requested by the king. As a result, Edward outlawed the clergy and excluded them from the royal protection. He violated the rights of the Church still further by seizing church property, taking into his hands the lay fees of the clergy of the province of Canterbury.[11]

Such legal difficulties between Church and State were destined to continue through the centuries, especially since the needs of the Church for temporal possessions became much greater. In the face of this progress the civil statutes became stricter, particularly in cases of alienation in mort-

[9] Statute 7 Edward I Statute *De Viris Religiosis*—Adams and Stephens, *Select Documents of English Constitutional History* (New York: Macmillan Company, 1916), p. 71 (hereafter cited as *Select Documents*).

[10] Statute 18 Edward I, c. 3—Adams and Stephens, *Select Documents*, p. 82.

[11] Stubbs, *The Constitutional History of England* (3 vols., Vol. II 3. ed., Oxford: The Clarendon Press, 1891), II, 135-136.

main. In 1391, during the reign of Richard II (1377-1399) the prohibition of alienation in mortmain was extended to all corporate bodies. The provisions of the statute were interpreted to forbid the contrivance of granting enfeoffment to laymen to the uses of religious houses and the acquisition of land by perpetual corporations such as guilds and fraternities.[12] Thus the law not only prevented all sales and gifts to religious houses but also all conveyance of land in trust for religious corporations except by permission of the crown. The statute ordered that all such uses should be changed into real titles or be sold to private persons, and that for the future lands sold in trust would be subject to forfeiture just as if the title had vested in the corporation; and the statute extended even to cemeteries that had been obtained under this device.[13]

Regardless of the Church's constant opposition to this infringement upon its inherent right to acquire, possess, own and administer property, independently of the State, the secular powers would not agree to allow land to become almost wholly inalienable as was the case, so they maintained, when it came into the Church's possession. In response to the objection that such legislation actually restricted freedom of alienation, State authorities always insisted that such was not the case. On the contrary, it was their contention that by thus restricting the Church's power of acquisition more property would fall into hands where it would be alienated more readily and more often, and therefore the freedom of alienation would be promoted rather than restricted.

Article III. Decrees of the V General Council of the Lateran and the Council of Trent

After the enactment of the first mortmain statutes there was no further statutory legislation affecting church prop-

[12] *Ibid.*, p. 509.

[13] Statute 15 Richard II, c. 5—Adams and Stephens, *op. cit.*, pp. 154-156.

erty in England until the reign of King Henry VIII (1509-1547). In some places, however, the civil authorities claimed a right to the ownership of tithes and first fruits which by law were to be dedicated to the uses of the Church. They appropriated churches and other ecclesiastical possessions, declaring that church property was no different from property held by their own subjects, but was to be acquired and held in accordance with the provisions of the civil law. The heresies of the sixteenth century and the subsequent political disturbances gave the enemies of the Church increased opportunities to confiscate ecclesiastical possessions. The first mortmain laws did not completely deny or forbid the right of the Church to acquire property, but rather limited the amount that could be obtained. With the advent of the Protestant Revolt, however, the very right to own and administer temporal goods was severely attacked.

The Church, anticipating these added difficulties in the V General Council of the Lateran (1512-1517), decreed that secular princes were forbidden to seize or to hold the income of churches, monasteries and benefices. It declared also that no civil authority was to hinder the beneficiary from obtaining possession of the fruits of his benefice. The Council based its legislation on principles of public law, asserting that the full administration and management of all ecclesiastical incomes belonged to the ecclesiastical authority, and that divine law forbade secular rulers to interfere in the disposition of church property.[14]

It was the Council of Trent (1545-1563), however, which manifested special concern for the rights of the Church regarding property matters. Convened to counteract the internal and external evils affecting the Church, its legislation was intended, among other things, to correct the flagrant abuses of usurpation aimed at ecclesiastical possessions. The Council directly admonished the secular princes of their duties, reminding them that God has willed that they be protectors of the holy faith and the Church.

[14] Hardouin, IX, 1756.

It exhorted them to allow the rights of the Church to be restored and to forbid their officials and magistrates, through any spirit of covetousness or impudence, to violate the immunity of the Church and of ecclesiastical persons, since such immunity has been established by the authority of God and the ordinances of the sacred canons. It reminded the secular authorities of their duties of obedience to the sacred constitutions of the supreme pontiffs and councils, ordaining and commanding that the decrees of the canons and of all the general councils regarding ecclesiastical persons and the liberty of the Church be accurately observed by all. The emperor, kings, states, princes, and all, of whatever state or dignity, and however bountifully they were adorned with temporal goods and with power over others, were exhorted to respect those things that were of ecclesiastical right and to look upon them as ordinances of God and as covered by his protection. They were urged to punish severely those who obstructed the Church's liberty, immunity and jurisdiction, especially those who were in any position of authority or influence. They were directed to be examples in the matter of piety, religion and protection of the churches.[15]

The canons of the Council also added sanctions to its decrees by inflicting penalties upon all violators. It declared the following:

> . . . if any cleric or layman, of whatever rank, even imperial or royal, should be so possessed by avarice, the root of all evil, as to presume to convert to his own use and to usurp *per se vel alios*, by force or fear, or even by means of supposititious persons, whether clerical or lay, or by any fraud or colored pretext whatsoever, the prerogatives, properties, rents and rights, even those held in fee or under lease, revenues, profits or any incomes

[15] Sess. XXV, *de ref.*, c. 20, *Quae sunt iuris ecclesiastici principibus saecularibus commendantur.* Use is made of the translation of the text of the Council by Schroeder (1875-1942) in his *Canons and Decrees of the Council of Trent* (St. Louis: B. Herder Book Co., 1941), pp. 517-518 (hereafter cited as Schroeder).

> whatsoever, belonging to any church or benefices, secular or regular, eleemosynary institutions or any other pious places, which ought to be used for the needs of the ministers and the poor, or to hinder them from being received by those to whom they by right belong, he shall be anathematized till he shall have restored integrally to the church and to its administrator or beneficiary the prerogatives, properties, effects, rights, fruits and revenues which he has seized or in whatever way they have come to him, even by way of gift from a supposititious person, and furthermore, till he shall have obtained absolution from the Roman Pontiff. If he be a patron of that church he shall, in addition to the aforesaid penalties, be *eo ipso* deprived of the right of patronage. The cleric who instigates or consents to an execrable fraud and usurpation of this kind shall be subject to the same penalties, and he shall be deprived of all benefices and be rendered unqualified to hold others; and even after complete satisfaction and absolution he shall be suspended, at the discretion of his ordinary, from the exercise of his orders.[16]

In regard to tithes that were due the Church, the Council spoke out against those who tried to appropriate them. It decreed as follows:

> Those are not to be tolerated who strive by various devices to withhold the tithes due to the churches, or who rashly take possession of and apply to their own use tithes to be paid by others, since the payment of tithes is due to God, and those who refuse to pay them or hinder those who pay them usurp the property of others. Therefore, the Holy Council commands all, of whatever rank or condition, on whom rests the obligation to pay tithes, that they in the future pay in full to the cathedral or to whatever other churches or persons to whom they are legitimately due, the tithes to which they are bound by law. Those who withhold them or hinder their payment shall be excommunicated, and they shall not be absolved

[16] Sess. XXII, *de ref.*, c. 11, *Bonorum cuiuscumque ecclesiae aut pii loci occupatores puniuntur*—Schroeder, pp. 430-431.

> from this crime until full restitution has been made. It further exhorts each and all, in Christian charity and the duty they owe their pastors, that they do not regard it a burden to assist liberally, out of the things given them by God, the bishops and priests who preside over the poorer churches, for the honor of God and the maintenance of the dignity of their pastors who watch over them.[17]

Article IV. The Legal Enactments of King Henry VIII and King Edward VI

The Council of Trent did not enact any new legislation regarding church property. It declared that it was restating and renewing all of the ordinances of former sacred canons and general councils which sought to protect the Church's immunity. The most flagrant violations of this immunity, however, had already been committed by King Henry VIII (1509-1547). It was in 1535 that Henry published the Act concerning the King's Highness to be Supreme Head of the Church of England, and to have authority to reform and redress all errors, heresies and abuses in the same.[18] This was the act whereby Henry attempted to transfer the papal jurisdiction to the imperial crown and declared that "the King, his heirs and successors, kings of this realm, shall be taken, accepted and reputed the only Supreme Head on earth of the Church of England, called *Anglicana Ecclesia*. . . ."[19] By Henry's legislation, "the religious belief of every Englishman was laid at the King's feet. He named the commissioners; he regulated their proceedings by his advice; he reviewed their decisions; and, if he confirmed them by letters patent under the Great Seal, they became, from that moment, the doctrines of the Eng-

[17] Sess. XXV, *de ref.*, c. 12, *Decimae integre persolvendae. Eas subtrahentes excommunicandi. Rectoribus ecclesiarum tenuium pie subveniendum.*—Schroeder, pp. 511-512.

[18] 26 Henry VIII, c. 1—Lilly and Wallis, *A Manual of the Law Specially Affecting Catholics* (London: William Clowes and Sons, 1893), p. 1 (hereafter cited as Lilly and Wallis).

[19] *Ibid.*, p. 3.

lish Church which every man was bound to believe under such penalties as might be assigned. . . ."[20]

With this condition existing in England, the temporal goods of the Church became the object of attack almost immediately. Henry began to seize church property by his mortmain statute, which was passed in 1531. It enacted that all future grants of lands to be held for superstitious uses, v.g., for Masses and the upkeep of shrines, should be void even if held by the heirs in trust, if such trusts were to endure for a period of more than twenty years.[21] By another statute entitled, "Concerning restraint of payment on annates to the See of Rome," it was enacted that if any prelate thereafter should presume to pay first fruits to the See of Rome, he should forfeit his personalties to the King, and the profits of his See as long as he held it, and that if the requisite Bulls for his consecration were, in consequence, denied, he might be consecrated without them; and it authorized the King to disregard any ecclesiastical censure of "our Holy Father, the Pope, or any of his successors," and to cause divine services to be continued in spite of the same.[22]

In 1536 Henry VIII began his extensive program of confiscation by dissolving what were known as the lesser monasteries or religious houses.[23] Three years later, by another statute, he dissolved the greater monasteries. The wording of the statute was similar to that of the first dissolution, with the emphasis placed upon the fact that everything "shall be vested, deemed, and adjudged by authority of this present parliament in the very actual and real seisin

[20] *Ibid.*, p. 15.

[21] Statute 23 Henry VIII, c. 10—Hannan, *The Canon Law of Wills*, The Catholic University of America Canon Law Studies, n. 86 (Washington D.C.: The Catholic University of America, 1934), p. 323, n. 548 (hereafter cited as Hannan).

[22] Statute 23 Henry VIII, c. 26—Lilly and Wallis, pp. 11-12.

[23] Statute 27 Henry VIII, c. 28—Adams and Stephens, *Select Documents*, pp. 244-245.

and possession of the king, our sovereign lord, his heirs and successors forever...."[24]

Henry VIII, by his Act of Supremacy, began the legal policy of religious discrimination. It was his intention to enforce uniformity of religion according to the doctrines of the Reformation and to repress all doctrines opposed to it. This was the ground on which all Catholic uses were held invalid for nearly three hundred years.[25] An example of this invalidation has been given above in a description of the Statute, 23 Henry VIII, c. 10, which forbade trusts of hereditaments to the use of parish churches, chapels, etc., for the purpose of having annual Masses offered, during any longer period than twenty years. There is no doubt that bequests for prayers and Masses for the benefit of the testator himself or other deceased persons were valid and enforced before the Reformation. Henry's restriction was the first to be placed upon them.[26] Later, however, Edward VI (1547-1553) in 1547 enacted the Statute of Chantries, which completed the work of discrimination by invalidating all such gifts without restriction. The statute asserted that property devoted to such superstitious purposes should be used to found schools and for other good purposes, and that the king should be entrusted with the execution of this design. It was established, therefore, that "lands, tenements and other hereditaments of every chantry, guild and fraternity, lands and tenements belonging to any chapel or stipendiary priests, shall be judged and deemed in the actual and real possession of our said sovereign lord the king, his heirs and successors forever, without any inquisition or office thereof to be had or found."[27]

[24] Statute 31 Henry VIII, c. 13—Stephenson and Marcham, *Sources of English Constitutional History* (New York and London: Harper & Brothers Publishers, 1937), pp. 317-318 (hereafter cited as Stephenson and Marcham).

[25] Cf. Lilly and Wallis, p. 143.

[26] *Ibid.*, p. 140.

[27] Statute 1 Edward 6, c. 14—Adams and Stephens, *Select Documents*, pp. 269-270.

It is to be noted that superstitious uses or purposes were specifically mentioned in the statutes of Henry VIII and Edward VI. A superstitious use, as thus referred to, was one which had for its object the propagation of the rites of a religion not tolerated by the law. Inasmuch as this statute prevented the Church from receiving the customary contributions of the faithful, whose offerings were considered to be for an illegal religious practice, it is evident how greatly the Acts of Conformity interfered with the inherent rights of the Church to acquire and administer property, and how severely the Church was to suffer as a consequence.

ARTICLE V. THE STATUTE, 43 ELIZABETH I, AND THE LATER STATUTES OF MORTMAIN

It has been explained that the mortmain laws were designed and enacted to prevent property from becoming permanently inalienable. The courts found it necessary to lay down rules to stop settlements which created what was in effect an unbarrable entail, or, as the lawyers of the sixteenth century and later called it, "a perpetuity." The civil legislators declared that, just as in the Middle Ages alienation into mortmain showed that landowners would, unless restrained, use their power to alienate freely so as to destroy that power, so also in later centuries the settlements attempted by them showed that they wished to do much the same thing by so tying up their land that no future owner would have complete power of alienation. Landowners adopted various devices to create perpetuities, and invariably rules were set up to frustrate this creation of unbarrable entails and settlements of property upon a succession of limited owners in perpetuity.[28]

Exceptions to the rule, however, were always made in favor of trusts and uses which the royal court judged it to be for the public benefit to perpetuate. Many of the purposes which the law thus favored were enumerated in

[28] Holdsworth, VII, 194.

the Statute, 43 Elizabeth I, c. 4. It was principally by means of that statute that a legal meaning was attached to the words, "charity," "charitable," "charitable uses," "charitable trusts," "charitable purposes." The preamble of the statute contained a list of charities so varied and so comprehensive that it became the practice of the Court to refer to it as a sort of index or chart.[29] The main purpose of 43 Elizabeth I, c. 4, was to define the uses which were charitable as distinguished from those which, after the Reformation in England, were deemed superstitious, and to secure their application. Under this statute courts of chancery were empowered to appoint commissioners to superintend the application and enforcement of charities; and if, from any cause, the charity could not be applied precisely as the testator had declared, such courts exercised the power of appropriating it in some cases, as nearly as they could to the purpose expressed and according to the principles indicated in the device.[30]

It is significant, however, that trusts for the support of religion were not mentioned in the Act of Elizabeth. Sir Francis More, in commenting on the statute in the reign of James I (1603-1625), asserted that such trusts had been purposely omitted, "lest," he said, "the gift intended to be employed upon purposes grounded upon charity might, in times of change (contrary to the minds of the givers) be confiscated into the king's treasury. For religion being variable, according to the pleasure of succeeding princes, that which at one time is held for orthodox may at another be accounted superstitious, and then such lands are confiscated as appears by the Statute of Chantries" (1 Edward 6, c. 14).[31] This opinion of Sir Francis More did not prevail inasmuch as trusts for the promotion of the established and then only legal religion were supported as within the equity of the statute, while trusts for the promotion and

[29] Lilly and Wallis, pp. 136-137.

[30] Bouvier, Law Dictionary and Concise Encyclopedia (2 vols. Vol. I 8.ed., St. Paul Minn., West Publishing Co., 1914), I, 462.

[31] Lilly and Wallis, p. 137.

aid of the Catholic religion were treated as illegal, and the money went to the crown to be applied to some legal charity. Thus not only was the intention of the testator defeated, but his money was often applied for the support of the Established Church.[32]

The Georgian Mortmain Act which was passed in 1735 imposed a restraint upon many of the charitable uses allowed by the Act of Elizabeth. It was enacted that no lands or tenements, nor money to be laid out thereon, should be given for or exchanged with any charitable uses, unless by deed indented, executed in the presence of two witnesses twelve calendar months before the death of the donor, and enrolled in the court of chancery within six months after its execution, taking effect immediately and without power.[33] Since the Catholic Religion, and therefore Catholic Charities, was already illegal at the time of this enactment it did not affect them. It was, however, to have an effect upon them at a later time when they finally were to receive recognition under the law.

This recognition of the Roman Catholic Religion began in 1788 when, by an act of parliament, there was passed the first Relief Act in favor of Roman Catholics. The statute was entitled, "An Act for relieving His Majesty's Subjects professing the Popish religion from certain penalties and disabilities imposed on them by an act made in the eleventh and twelfth years of the reign of King William the Third."[34] In 1791 a similar statute was passed, entitled, "An Act to relieve, upon conditions, and under restrictions, the persons therein described from certain penalties and disabilities to which Papists or persons professing the Popish religion are by law subject."[35] By this Relief Act the Catholic religion ceased to be unlawful, but an *ex pro-*

[32] *Ibid.*, pp. 137-138.

[33] Statute 9 George II, c. 36—Hannan, p. 323, n. 549.

[34] Statute 18 George III, c. 60—Wharton, *The Statute Law now in Force Relating to Roman Catholics in England* (London: Spettigue and Farrance Co., 1851), pp. 118-119 (hereafter cited as Wharton).

[35] Statute 31 George III, c. 32—Wharton, p. 123.

viso in the 17th section of the Act stated that whatever uses, trusts and dispositions of real or personal property were theretofore deemed superstitious or unlawful should continue to be so deemed, notwithstanding that Act.[36]

In 1832 there was enacted the Roman Catholic Charities Act. Its full title was, "An Act for the better securing the charitable donations and bequests of His Majesty's subjects in Great Britain professing the Roman Catholic Religion."[37] The measure of freedom granted by this Act was truly considered a relief when compared to the former status of ecclesiastical property, but it was by no means in conformity with the full rights which the Popes and Councils had decreed as belonging to the Church, for although trusts for Catholic purposes were held good, there were still those exceptions which placed an unjust restraint upon the Church's potential temporal goods. If the Court did not consider a certain trust as having a charitable purpose, it ruled that trust void. Likewise, if the Court decided that a trust was for superstitious uses or for the support of forbidden religious orders which it wished to suppress, it was deemed unlawful.[38]

The difficulties imposed by the law regarding trusts and bequests for Masses and for the religious orders were lessened to some degree in 1860 by the Statute, 23 & 24 Victoria. The Act provided that no existing or future gift or disposition of real or personal estate upon any lawful charitable trust for the exclusive benefit of persons professing the Roman Catholic Religion shall be invalidated by reason *only* that the same estate has been or shall be also subjected to any trust or provision deemed to be superstitious or otherwise prohibited by the laws affecting persons professing the same religion, but in every such case it shall be lawful for the High Court of Chancery or any judge thereof . . . to apportion the same estate or the an-

[36] Cf. Lilly and Wallis, p. 138.
[37] Statute 2 & 3 William IV, c. 115—Wharton, pp. 166-167.
[38] Lilly and Wallis, p. 139.

nual income or benefit thereof. . . ."[39] It is to be noted that this Act did not apply when a bequest was entirely devoted to an unlawful purpose, but only when some of the purposes were lawful and some unlawful. In such a case the bequest was to be apportioned, with part assigned for the lawful purposes mentioned in the will, and the remaining part being devoted to some lawful Catholic Charity.[40]

An important alteration of the Mortmain Act was made in 1891, so that the Church could acquire property through charitable bequests in wills. It was called the Mortmain and Charitable Uses Act. Before the passing of this Act, testators, while free to bequeath their personal property to lawful charitable uses, were absolutely restrained from doing so with land, or personal property connected with land and known as impure personalty, such as leaseholds, mortgages, etc., and such bequests were illegal and void; but by the Act of 1891, in the case of all persons dying after the passing of that Act, it was allowed that "land may be assured by will to or for the benefit of any charitable use, but, except as hereinafter provided, such land shall, notwithstanding anything in the will contained to the contrary, be sold within one year from the death of the testator."[41]

While it is true that this Act at least prevented the testator's intention from failing for want or compliance with the Mortmain Acts, and that the Church could thus benefit thereby, nevertheless the bequest still continued to be affected with troublesome and uncertain conditions, which made the authorities of the Church cautious and careful to advise landowners, who were desirous of leaving something to the Church, to convey their land to trustees during lifetime, or to direct their charitable legacies to be paid out of their personal estate, other than leaseholds.

[39] *Ibid.*, p. 148.
[40] *Loc. cit.*
[41] Statute 54 & 55 Victoria, c. 73—Lilly and Wallis, p. 154.

Article VI. Decrees of the Church in the Eighteenth and Nineteenth Centuries

During the centuries following the outbreak of the Protestant Revolt, and in recent centuries, the Church has continued to defend its property rights and to define repeatedly its traditional teaching in this matter. Pope Clement XIII (1758-1769), in his Constitution *Alias ad Apostolatus* (1768), condemned a series of edicts which forbade, or in some degree limited, the transfer of the use of ownership of property to ecclesiastical hands. Although the edicts did not openly deny the Church's right to acquire property, the presumption was that such a right was subject to the secular powers, which sought to appoint laymen to administer church property and to supervise the payment of church revenues. Pope Clement decreed that such edicts prejudiced the liberty, immunity and rights of the Church.[42]

In the Council of Lyons (1850) the bishops restated the inherent right of the Church regarding temporal goods. They declared the fundamental principle that the Church, as a visible, perfect society of divine origin, is essentially capable of ownership and of all acts of administration.[43]

Pope Pius IX (1846-1878) spoke out authoritatively on many occasions to defend ecclesiastical possessions. In his allocution *Quibus luctuosissimis* (1851) he used language similar to that of the present Code of Canon Law, and voiced the traditional teaching of the Church as set forth from its beginning.[44] In another allocution, *Nemo Vestrum* (1855), he condemned the decrees of the Spanish Cortes, which violated a concordat between Spain and the Holy See by ordering the confiscation and sale of church prop-

[42] *Codicis Iuris Canonici Fontes,* cura Emi Petri Card. Gasparri editi (9 vols., Romae; *Typis Polyglottis Vaticanis,* 1923-1939: Vols. VII-IX, ed., cura et studio Emi Iustiniani Card. Serédi), v. 464 (hereafter cited as Fontes).

[43] *Acta et Decreta Sacrorum Conciliorum Recentiorum, Collectio Lacensis* (7 vols., Friburgi Brisgoviae, 1870-1890), IV, 481, c. 23 (hereafter cited as *Coll. Lac*).

[44] *Fontes,* n. 512.

erty. He stated that such actions were a usurpation of the patrimony of the Church and thus contrary to divine and human law.[45]

In Italy the rise of Nationalism and Liberalism endangered the possessions of the Church and actually resulted in the seizure of part of the Papal States. Pius IX, in this allocution *Iamdudum cernimus* (1861), again defended the rights of the Church by declaring the seizure an unjust usurpation of the Church's just possessions.[46] He stated that those who commit such usurpation act sacrilegiously against the laws and rights of the Church, for they reject its personality as a perfect society and make it subject to the sovereignty of the State.[47] In his *Syllabus errorum* (1864) he condemned the proposition which denied the Church the right to acquire and possess property.[48] Finally, by means of two encyclicals, Pius IX condemned the civil laws which usurped and secularized church property. He declared that Christ had endowed His Church with the right and the capacity to acquire temporal goods, and that the exercise of that right does not depend upon the good pleasure of the secular authority, nor does it usurp or encroach upon the rights of the civil powers. He condemned the error which taught that the ownership of all church property was in the hands of the State.[49]

The bishops, united in the General Council of the Vatican (1869-1870), issued a decree upholding the rights of the Church in property matters. They stated:

> We teach that the Church, as a visible society established by God among men, has the right to acquire and to possess temporal goods and cannot be deprived of that right by any secular power.

[45] *Acta Pii Papae IX, ex quibus excerptus est Syllabus* (Romae, Typis Rev. Camerae Apostolicae, 1865), pp. 136-140.

[46] *Ibid.*, pp. 196-203.

[47] *Ibid.*, (*Allocut.*, *Maxima quidem*, 1862), pp. 210-218; *Allocut.*, *Universus catholicus orbis*, 1867—Fontes, n. 547.

[48] *Prop.* 26—*Fontes*, n. 543.

[49] Encycl. *Incredible*, 1863—*Fontes*, n. 537; Encycl. *Quanta cura*, 1864—Fontes, n. 542.

> Moreover . . . we declare that the laws according to which the political state, as if by supreme inherent right, usurps ecclesiastical property are unjust spoliations.[50]

Pope Leo XIII (1878-1903), in his encyclical *Immortale Dei* (1885), set forth the rights of the Church as prerogatives which are free and independent from the State. He insisted that the State does not have an absolute or unlimited control over temporal goods, and that the civil powers may not interfere with the Church's property rights.[51]

In 1905 the French Government enacted its law of Church and State separation. As a result the Church was no longer recognized as a legal personality, and all of its property was to be taken over and administered by associations of laymen; otherwise it was to be confiscated and given to community charities. Pope Pius X (1903-1914) condemned this denial of the basic rights of the Church in his allocution *Gravissimum* (1906), and in the two encyclical letters, *Vehementer Nos* (1906) and *Une fois encore* (1907).[52]

In all of its decrees it has always been the policy of the Church to state its rights prudently, to have the civil power recognize them, and to safeguard them with the protection of the civil law. The claim of the Church is always the same: it possesses the native right, independently of the secular power, to acquire, hold and administer temporal goods in the achievement of its holy purpose.

[50] *Coll. Lac.*, VII, 576.
[51] *Fontes*, n. 592.
[52] *Fontes*, nn. 671, 672, 677.

CHAPTER III

LEGISLATION OF THE CHURCH AND THE STATE IN THE UNITED STATES

Article I. The American Colonies

During the early period of the American colonies the Church suffered opposition and faced difficulties quite similar to those in England. Since English legislation also governed the colonies, efforts were made to legally exclude Catholics. The Anglican Church was officially established in the southern colonies. The charter of the colony of Virginia (1609) expressed the displeasure of the King of England toward admitting any Catholics who would not take the oath of Supremacy. In 1629 when the Catholic, Lord Baltimore († 1632), attempted to enter the colony the provisions of the charter were applied and he was excluded. In 1642 there was passed an act by which Catholics coming into Virginia were disfranchised, and priests were to be expelled within five days. Another act of 1699 renewed the privation of the franchise to all "Popish recusants."[1]

In the southern area, which is now North and South Carolina and Georgia, the situation was substantially the same. In 1696 a toleration act was passed allowing all Christians complete freedom of conscience. Only Catholics, i.e., Papists, were excepted. By an act of 1715 Catholics were excluded from the franchise in the Carolinas.[2] In the New England group of colonies, where Congregationalism prevailed, there was instituted a program to exclude all who did not conform to Congregationalist ideas. In 1647 a law was passed by Massachusetts forbidding Jesuits

[1] Dignan, *Catholic Church Property: A History of the Legal Incorporation of Catholic Church Property in the United States* (New York: P. J. Kenedy & Sons, 1935), pp. 2-3 (hereafter cited as Dignan).

[2] *Loc. cit.*

and priests to enter that colony, and it directed that those who came were to be banished immediately. In 1691 Massachusetts received a new charter making the English Toleration Act lawful, but again Catholics were excepted. The same act was promulgated in 1689 in New York, and in 1702 in the Jerseys.[3] Although legal discrimination was practiced also in Maryland and Pennsylvania, greater freedom was granted to Catholics in those colonies than in all others. In Pennsylvania the Church was successful in acquiring property as early as the first half of the eighteenth century, the lands being held in the name of an individual priest.[4]

In the Colony of Maryland Catholics were actually given a legal status, and one of the remarkable features of the charter was the deliberate exclusion of the English Mortmain law, *Quia emptores terrarum.* Complete authority was given to Lord Baltimore to transfer real property to all who wished to purchase it. By the provisions of the Conditions of Plantation lands were given to the Jesuit Society for the support of the priests sent to the colony from England. These lands were held in fee simple in conformity with the rights of other colonists.[5]

Later, however, restrictions were placed upon the tenure of property. In 1638 legislation was passed whereby all landed property was to be held by the colonists as a fief. It forbade transfers and conveyances of property except through reversion to the Proprietor. In 1641 the statute of mortmain was revived, so that it became forbidden for both ecclesiastical and temporal corporations, societies and other groups to acquire or inherit any land in the colony without the special permission of Lord Baltimore. All persons were made incapable of giving lands to such groups or of holding it in trust for them. To secure what property they held, the Jesuits found it necessary sometimes to inter-

[3] *Ibid.*, pp. 16, 17, 25, 29.
[4] *Ibid.*, p. 32.
[5] *Ibid.*, pp. 33-35.

pose a reliable Catholic layman as trustee between the civil authority and the church property. During the seventeenth and eighteenth centuries, titles were vested either in laymen or individuals belonging to the Order, and they were heavily bonded to insure the execution of the trust.[6] It was in this way that the Church managed to retain possession of its temporal goods amid periodic waves of bitter opposition until after the War of Independence, when gradually the principle of religious equality was admitted by the individual states.

ARTICLE II. THE PLENARY COUNCILS OF BALTIMORE

In the United States after the advent of religious freedom the Church expressed and defended its property rights through the Plenary Councils of Baltimore. The I Plenary Council (1852) decreed that whatever is given to God for divine worship passes under the dominion of the Church. It strictly forbade laymen to interfere in the administration of ecclesiastical goods without permission of the bishop, and declared that the penalties inflicted by the Council of Trent would be incurred *ipso facto* by those who diverted such goods to their own uses or frustrated and defrauded the will of the donors.[7]

The Pastoral Letter issued by the Council gave a clear statement of the canonical principles governing church property. From the wording of the letter it is evident that the Church's chief concern regarding property was not so much in its relation with the secular authority but rather with the correction of internal abuses. The evil of trusteeism had become an outstanding difficulty for the Church as a result of the pretensions of a rebellious laity to control ecclesiastical possessions. It resulted in the encroachment of lay influences upon the spiritual jurisdiction of the

[6] *Ibid.*, pp. 36-39.

[7] *Concilium Plenarium Totius Americae Septentrionalis Foederatae, Baltimori Tributum,* (Baltimori: Apud Joannem Murphy et Socios, 1852), p. 47. This was decree No. 16 of the Council.

priests and bishops, and in a wrong concept of the right of patronage, to which unruly trustees laid claim. Thus the Church's problem was to secure a legal and satisfactory method of safeguarding its property.[8]

When the II Plenary Council of Baltimore convened in 1866, it issued a clear and complete statement of the Church's rights regarding the tenure and administration of property.[9] Archbishop Spalding, the Apostolic Delegate to the Council, wished to publish a "complete repertory of our canon law embracing, in systematic order, all of our previous enactments in the Baltimore Councils together with such canons of provincial and diocesan synods as we may wish to make of general application; in a word, of making it a sort of *corpus iuris* for the American Church; throwing into an appendix all Roman rescripts and decisions which have reference to our affairs. . . ."

A difficult situation had arisen inasmuch as the condition of the civil laws varied greatly from state to state regarding the manner in which the bishops were allowed to hold property. It was necessary, therefore, to clarify the civil and canonical principles involved. The Council issued a Pastoral Letter in which it reminded the people that in some states the Church was still forbidden to safeguard its property in conformity with its discipline. Attention was called to the fact that such states did not recognize the Church in its corporate capacity, and thus imposed upon it a system of tenure which was alien to its principles and which was borrowed from those who had rejected its authority. It was declared that the actions of those states were an expression of a distrust of ecclesiastical power and the fruit of the misrepresentations which had been made of the Church in the past ages.[10]

[8] Cf. Guilday, *A History of the Councils of Baltimore* (New York: The Macmillan Co., 1932), pp. 38, 59, 87.

[9] *Concilii Plenarii Baltimorensis II, In Ecclesia Metropolitana Baltimorensi Acta et Decreta,* (Baltimorae: Joannes Murphy, 1868), Decrees nn. 182-188, pp. 111-113.

[10] Dignan, pp. 195, 212-213.

On November 6, 1884, the III Plenary Council of Baltimore assembled. It reaffirmed the decrees of the II Plenary Council and emphasized the right of the Church, as a self-sufficient society, on the basis of the natural law itself, to possess property for the fulfillment of its mission upon earth. It directed which methods of tenure were to be adopted, according to the legislation of the individual states, to secure church property in the safest manner possible. The Council made it clearly understood that no matter how the legal title to church property may be held, "it always remains true that the properties are held in trust for the Church for the benefit of the people." Bishops were directed to distinguish carefully between their personal possessions and those of the diocese, and they were ordered to keep a double inventory, one of which was to list all of the church property which they held in fee simple, in trust, or as corporations sole, and the other, their personal property. They were obliged in conscience to draw up a will in duplicate, or some other legal document, to secure the transmission of church property to their successors; and since the security of the property depended upon the requirements of the civil laws, care was to be taken that all of the formalities required by the latter were observed.[11]

Article III. Decrees of the Sacred Congregation of the Council

The legislation of the Councils of Baltimore produced the good results of making church authorities careful about securing church property in the safest manner possible in keeping with the legal provisions of the individual states. The Councils, however, had very little influence upon the civil legislation as such. Although the mortmain statutes were not enacted in the United States, with the exception of the State of Pennsylvania, nevertheless their influence has

[11] *Acta et Decreta Concilii Plenarii Baltimorensis Tertii In Ecclesia Metropolitana Baltimorensi Habiti a die IX Novembris usque ad diem VII Decembris A.D. 1886,* (Baltimorae: Typis Joannis Murphy et Soc., nn. 264-270, pp. 149-155.

been quite evident in the restraining measures passed against the Church's property rights. Such measures have not been in full accord with religious freedom as guaranteed by the first amendment of the Constitution.

Since the states do not recognize the juridical personality of the Church with its consequent inherent right to acquire and administer property, the Church has held its temporal goods by way of several different methods recognized by the civil law. The three most common methods have been corporation sole, corporation aggregate, and fee simple.

In 1911, the Sacred Congregation of the Council issued an instruction concerning the manner of holding church property in the United States. It directed that the method of fee simple, whereby a bishop holds and administers all of the goods in his own name by an absolute and full legal title, was to be abolished.[12] Doheny has noted the good reasons for abandoning such a method. He pointed out that property held in fee simple was oftentimes subject to taxation in this country; secondly, in the event of bankruptcy the entire church property of a diocese could be assigned to the creditors; thirdly, the bishop was liable for all debts of the various parishes; fourthly, wills had to be made for the proper transfer of the church property, and these could be broken or contested; fifthly, in the interim between the death of one bishop and the appointment of a successor everything was in utter confusion; sixthly, inheritance taxes were often exacted, which meant an undue burden especially in the poorer dioceses; finally, property willed to the bishop after his death could be claimed by the Church only with the greatest difficulty in many states.[13]

Tenure of property by bishops as corporations sole was not forbidden by the decree of 1911, but there was ex-

[12] S. C. C. 29 iul. 1911—*Eccles. Review*, XLV (1911), 585.

[13] Doheny, *Church Property: Modes of Acquisition*, The Catholic University of America Canon Law Studies, n. 41 (Washington, D.C.: The Catholic University of America, 1927), p. 41. (hereafter cited *Church Property*)

pressed a preference for the corporation aggregate method if such a system was recognized and protected by the laws of the State. Under such a system the church property is vested in a body corporate formed from a group of members of the society thus incorporated. The incorporators hold the property under their control, but their possession is the possession of the artificial person whose agents they are. They have a voice in the management of the property, but this right is an authority, and not an estate or title. Thus the rights of the clergy and the power of the bishops are not jeopardized, and at the same time the laity can be represented. The property remains safe from the dangers of the fee simple method, for the death of a trustee does not affect the life of the corporation. Above all, the authority of the Church remains intact through the clergy, who retain the controlling power in the management of the property.[14]

[14] *Ibid.*, pp. 39-40.

Part II

PROPERTY LEGISLATION IN CANON LAW AND THE CIVIL LAW OF OHIO

CHAPTER IV

THE ACQUISITION AND TENURE OF CHURCH PROPERTY IN CANON LAW

The foregoing historical synopsis has presented a consideration of some of the chief problems which the Church has encountered through the ages in acquiring, holding and administering the property necessary for the successful achievement of its divinely appointed purpose upon earth. In our own age there exist similar problems, the nature of which is determined by the laws and customs of each country or locality. In the United States and in the individual states there has been enacted legislation which affects church property favorably or unfavorably, depending upon the extent in which it conforms to or diverges from the canons and decrees of the Church. Since the State of Ohio, existing as a sovereignty in its own right, is the primary concern of this comparative study, it will be necessary to examine, together with the Church's legislation, the constitution and the laws of Ohio insofar as they are parallel or not to the provisions of the present Code of Canon Law.

ARTICLE I. THE RIGHT OF THE CHURCH TO ACQUIRE AND HOLD PROPERTY

In that section of the Code which treats of temporal goods or possessions the Church makes a specific mention of state authority. Canon 1495, § 1, states that the Church has an inherent right to acquire, to own and to administer property for the attainment of its end or purpose. Since it is a native right, the Church is careful to declare in the same canon that it holds that right freely and independently of any civil authority.[1] To have such a right freely, as ex-

[1] *"Ecclesia catholica et Apostolica Sedes nativum ius habent libere et independenter a civili potestate acquirendi, retinendi et administrandi bona temporalia ad fines sibi proprios prosequendos."*

pressed in the canon, indicates that the Church, in obtaining and owning its property, is not subject to the imposition of burdens by the civil law. The independence claimed by the Church in this same canon negates the necessity of legal recognition by the civil power and the need of any legal permission on the part of the State.[2]

In laying claim to its native right regarding temporal possessions, the Church merely repeats what it has stated from the time of its divine institution by Christ. Many of the declarations, decrees and condemnations made by ecclesiastical authorities to vindicate the Church's rights have been quoted in the first part of this study. We have seen how necessary it has been for the Church to defend its position in the many conflicts it has waged with heretics and other usurpers of ecclesiastical goods. In all such instances it has set forth substantially the same vigorous statement which is employed in the present Code.

The inherent right which is stated in Canon 1495, § 1, is based upon the Church's God-given nature as a self-sufficient society. According to the wording of the canon, it is from the Creator Himself that the Church has received all of the prerogatives necessary for the accomplishment of its spiritual purpose. Among those prerogatives is included the right of holding property which aids its ministers to exercise successfully their spiritual and temporal duties toward all of its members.[3] Since the Church has been instituted thus by divine ordinance, it is not dependent upon any human authority in its power and capacity to exercise its rights. It transcends the range of civil rights conferred by any particular system of jurisprudence.[4]

[2] Cappello, *Summa Iuris Canonici* (3 vols., Vol, II, 4. ed., Romae: *Apud Aedes Universitatis Gregorianae*, 1945), II, p. 546, n. 572.

[3] De Meester, *Iuris Canonici et Iuris Canonico-civilis Compendium* (nova editio, 3 vols. in 4, Brugis: Desclée, 1921-28), III, nos. 1438-44.

[4] Brown, *The Canonical Juristic Personality with Special Reference to its Status in the United States of America*, The Catholic University of America Canon Law Studies, n. 39 (Washington, D.C.: The Catholic University of America, 1927), pp. 90, 91 (hereafter cited as *The Canonical Juristic Personality*).

The Catholic Church and the Apostolic See, therefore, have been endowed from the beginning with the essential character of moral persons, (i.e., corporations).[5] Such juridical personality is necessary in order that the Church may claim the right to temporal goods, since property is something that belongs exclusively and properly to a person.[6] The expression, "Catholic Church," as used in Canon 1495, § 1, is understood to mean the visible and perfect society founded by Christ and instituted as a juridical person. The expression, "Apostolic See," according to Canon 7, includes not only the Roman Pontiff but the Roman Curia as well, consisting of the Congregations, Tribunals and Offices.[7] Both Church and State recognize the existence of such persons as can be distinguished from individual physical persons or rational beings. In the days of Roman jurisprudence, as well as at the present time, moral persons have been instituted by the civil law as juridical entities, and they have been given definite rights and duties by the authority which gave them existence. One of the important concerns of Canon 1495, § 1, however, is to establish the fact that the Church's personality and rights in property matters depend not upon the civil authority as their author, but upon God alone. This truth expressed in the canon can be demonstrated especially through the demands inherent in the natural divine law, through the precepts enacted in the positive divine law, and through the constant practice of the Church.

By virtue of the natural divine law, society in general, or any particular society, has a duty to profess a true religious belief through its worship of God externally and

[5] Can. 100. This canon gives the basis for Canon 1495 when it states that "Catholica Ecclesia et Apostolica Sedes moralis personae rationem habent ex ipsa ordinatione divina;..."

[6] Goodwine, *The Right of the Church to Acquire Temporal Goods*, The Catholic University of America Canon Law Studies, n. 131 (Washington, D.C.: The Catholic University of America Press, 1941), pp. 1, 2.

[7] Cf. Doheny, *Church Property;* p. 26.

publicly. God, the Creator of individual men, is also the Author of society and requires that it recognize His authority and observe His laws.[8] This obligation toward the Creator, however, implies a corresponding right. If a society, such as the Church, is to function successfully, in keeping with the purpose of its existence which is the worship of God and the salvation of souls, it must have a secure right to acquire and to use all of the licit means necessary for its life and activity. But the Church, like all other associations of men, has a need for temporal goods or property to enable it to function effectively as an external and visible society. The right to its life and to the preservation of its life belongs to the Church as a moral person, even as such a right belongs to every physical person. As an honorable and beneficial society the Church cannot perform its acts of worship, undertake its works of charity, or conduct its programs of instruction and propagation of the Faith without buildings, institutions and a great variety of material resources.[9]

Since God, and not civil authority has given the Church its existence and its right to exist, it is also from the divine will that the Church has received its right to maintain its existence and thus to acquire and own property. It is, therefore, *de iure* a society which is wholly independent of the State and supreme in its own domain.[10]

The positive divine law confirms these principles by the manner in which Christ, as God, instituted the Church. As the Divine Author of both Church and State, He did not designate one to be either subservient to or dependent

[8] Tanquerey, *Synopsis Theologicae Dogmaticae* (3 vols., Vol. II, 24. ed., Parisiis, Desclée, 1937), II, pp. 113, 114, nos. 167, 168.

[9] Ottaviani, *Institutiones Iuris Publici Ecclesiastici* (2 vols., Vol. I, 4.ed., *Romae: Typis Polyglottis Vaticanis,* 1947) I, pp. 367, 368, 369, n. 198; Vromant, *De Bonis Ecclesiae Temporalibus* (Louvain: Museum Lessianum, 1927), p. 2, n. 1.

[10] Goodwine, *The Right of the Church to Acquire Temporal Goods,* p. 7.

on the other in any way.[11] It was His will that the two societies differ in their end and purpose, each being self-sufficient and supreme in its own sphere of activity. Christ gave to the Church the commission of helping man toward salvation, a task which is beyond the power and capacity of the State. In appointing the authority to rule the Church in the achievement of its end, Christ made no allusion to civil authority, but He invested one man with full power of binding and loosing, absolutely, universally and independently.[12] This fullness of authority necessarily includes all of the rights needed by the Church, as a moral person, to function as a sovereignty distinct and separate from the State. The right to acquire, own and administer property, therefore, belongs to the Church, not by any concession or permission of the civil society, but by a direct grant of the Divine Founder Himself.[13]

In the foregoing chapters of the historical synopsis it has been demonstrated how constant has been the practice of the Church to acquire temporal goods, even in the face of opposition on the part of the secular powers. It has been seen that, when the Church was first established, civil rulers not only opposed its appearance upon earth, but were openly resentful of the authority and rights which it claimed. Regardless of this opposition, it is certain that the early Christians acquired property, though there is no certainty about the precise manner in which they held it.[14] After the Edict of Milan, however, formal recognition was given to the Church's rights in property matters, and in many instances the Church was exceptionally favored with special privileges. At that time it was universally accepted that the Church held property in its own right. This independ-

[11] Pistocchi, *De Bonis Ecclesiae Temporalibus*, (Taurini: Marietti 1932), p. 14.

[12] Matthew: XII, 18-19; Goodwine, *The Right of the Church to Acquire Temporal Goods*, pp. 45, 46.

[13] Ottaviani, *Institutiones Iuris Publici Ecclesiastici*, I, p. 369, n. 199.

[14] Eusebius, *Historia Eccl.* Lib. VI, cap. 43—MPG, XX, 622.

ence was confirmed by the fact that the Church never requested the State to confer such a right upon it, nor did the civil authority consider it necessary to do so.[15]

Article II. The Right of Subordinate Ecclesiastical Moral Persons

Canons 99 and 100 of the present Code declare the existence of other ecclesiastical moral persons besides the Universal Church and the Apostolic See.[16] These juridical entities are described as being inferior or subordinate persons inasmuch as they depend upon an act of ecclesiastical authority for their existence and recognition (can. 100, § 1) and for the validity of their acts. The legislator has divided such persons into two general classifications—collegiate and non-collegiate. Collegiate moral persons consist of corporate bodies of physical persons, such as religious communities. Non-corporate or non-collegiate moral persons have property as their basic substratum, and they comprise all other institutions legally established by the Church as, for example, seminaries, benefices, or individual churches.[17] Whereas the Code gives this description of subordinate juristic persons and authorizes their existence, it does not

[15] Bartlett, *The Tenure of Parochial Property in the United States of America,* The Catholic University of America Canon Law Studies, n. 31 (Washington D.C.: The Catholic University of America, 1926), p. 7 (hereafter cited as *The Tenure of Parochial Property*).

[16] Can. 99—In Ecclesia, praeter personas physicas, sunt etiam personae morales, publica auctoritate constitutae, quae distinguuntur in personas morales collegiales et non collegiales, ut ecclesiae, Seminaria, beneficia, etc.

Can. 100. § 1. Catholica Ecclesia et Apostolica Sedes moralis personae rationem habent ex ipsa ordinatione divina; ceterae inferiores personae morales in Ecclesia eam sortiuntur sive ex ipso iuris praescripto sive ex speciali competentis Superioris ecclesiastici concessione data per formale decretum ad finem religiosum vel caritativum.

Can. 100, § 2—Persona moralis collegialis constitui non potest, nisi ex tribus saltem personis physicis.

Can. 100, § 3—Personae morales sive collegiales sive not collegiales minoribus aequiparantur.

[17] Can. 99.

offer a precise definition. They are usually spoken of, however, as being within the Church, all such legal entities other than physical persons, which have the capacity of acquiring and of exercising rights according to the provisions of the sacred canons.[18]

It is canonically established, therefore, that ecclesiastical personality, or the power to acquire and exercise rights in the Church, may be conferred upon corporate bodies and institutions by public ecclesiastical authority, just as it is granted to physical persons through the reception of baptism. The second paragraph of canon 1495 invests these subordinate corporations with the right of acquiring, holding and administering temporal goods in the same manner as the Church Universal and the Apostolic See. This is not a native right, however, for such corporations are parts of the entire Church, and they must depend upon its authority in the fulfillment of their ends and in the choice of means. The exercise of their property rights is valid only after they have derived their legal personality from the Church through a provision of law or a charter from a competent ecclesiastical superior. This provision or charter must be given by way of a formal decree of establishment. Moreover, the purpose of the legal person must be a religious or charitable one.[19]

The existence of subordinate ecclesiastical persons is necessary if the Church is to achieve its divine purpose. As a self-sufficient society it must make use of such means, and this has been the practice of the Church from its earliest days. Eusebius stated that parishes and other legal corporations were aware of their capacity and right, through their administrators to acquire property.[20] They realized, however, that they were responsible to an ecclesiastical superior for their acts of acquisition and that they retained their rights only if they remained in union with

[18] Blat, *Commentarium Textus Codicis Iuris Canonici* (5 vols., Vol. II, Romae, 1919) II, 28 (hereafter cited as Blat).

[19] Canon 100, § 1.

[20] *Historia Eccl.,* Lit. X, cap. 5, *MPG,* XX, 883.

the Church Universal.[21] Present-day legislation remains the same. Dissident parishes and schismatic corporations forfeit their right to acquire church property or to retain the property acquired while a corporate member of the Church. By schism they cease to be organic members of the fold. As a result they lose their legal personality and their property reverts to the Church.[22]

Subordinate ecclesiastical persons perform their legal acts, in property matters, through agents or administrators appointed by the competent authority. Some administrators are empowered to act in their own name and according to their own discretion in representing the collegiate person. The decisions which these representatives make and the acts performed by them within the scope of their authority are considered as the acts of the corporation itself.[23]

Article III. Kinds of Property

Property which the Church acquires and administers, in the exercise of its rights, is referred to by the Code as *bona ecclesiastica.* This term is used regardless of whether the property is held by the Church Universal, by the Apostolic See, or by any other ecclesiastical moral person.[24] It is, therefore, the temporal goods coming under this classification that are subject to the provisions of the sacred canons. Having been obtained by some legitimate means

[21] Vromant, De Bonis Ecclesiae Temporalibus (3. ed., Louvain: Museum Lessianum, 1953, p. 23, n. 16.

[22] Doheny, *Church Property,* p. 29; Cf. Case of Paul of Samasota: Eusebius, *Hist. Eccl.,* Lit. VII, Cf. 30, n. 19—MPG, XX, 719: In this case, after Paul had been deposed by the Synod of Antioch (268), he refused to give up the episcopal residence and the other church property. The orthodox element appealed to the Emperor, who decided that the property should be restored to those who were in communion with the Bishop of Rome.

[23] Brown, *The Canonical Juristic Personality,* pp. 99-100.

[24] Can. 1497, § 1. Bona temporalia, sive corporalia, tum immobilia tum mobilia, sive incorporalia, quae vel ad Ecclesiam universam et ad Apostolicam Sedem vel ad aliam in Ecclesia personam moralem pertineant, sunt *bona ecclesiastica.*

of acquisition, all such property is thereby set apart to be used in the achievement of the Church's supernatural end.

Canon 1497, § 1, divides ecclesiastical property into that which is corporeal, both movable and immovable, and that which is incorporeal. If the temporal goods come within the perception of the senses they are classified as corporeal. If corporeal goods are of a kind that one cannot move them from place to place without affecting their integrity, they are called immovable. All other corporeal goods come under the category of movable property.[25]

A further classification of ecclesiastical possessions separates them into goods that have been set apart from other property by way of a consecration or a blessing, or goods which have a special, historical and artistic value attached to them, or a value that derives through rare workmanship or material as distinguished from ordinary property. If the property has been blessed or consecrated and is thereby especially dedicated to the activity of divine worship, it enjoys immunity from profane uses and is referred to as a *res sacra.* If its value is based upon some one of the other reasons stated above, it is called a *res pretiosa.*[26]

It is evident, therefore, that the right of the Church to temporal goods extends to all kinds of property without exception. The Church finds such property necessary or useful in accomplishing its divinely established mission. Since the divine act of creation furnishes any society with the material means for its purposes, the Church as a self-sufficient society cannot be restricted in the possession of what it must use for the work of saving souls.

Article IV. Modes of Acquisition and Manner of Tenure

Ownership of property postulates in the prospective owner a certain inherent capacity for possession. It postulates

[25] Vromant, *De Bonis Ecclesiae Temporalibus,* p. 47, n. 36.

[26] Can. 1497, § 2. Dicuntur *sacra,* quae consecratione vel benedictione ad divinum cultum destinata sunt; *pretiosa,* quibus notabilis valor sit, artis vel historiae vel materiae causa. Cf. Doheny, *Church Property,* pp. 31, 32.

also that the property be something which can be owned by the subject in the accomplishment of an end or purpose. In assuming ownership there must be a legal title which is surrendered by one person in transferring the property, and obtained by another person in acquiring it. Finally, it is necessary that definitely established means be available by which property can effectively and manifestly be transferred from one person to another.[27]

The Code, therefore, states the Church's right to acquire property through all of the just means which the natural and positive law sanctions for others.[28] In § 2 of canon 1499 the Church settles the question of proprietary rights of juristic persons. It is definitely determined that ownership of property is vested in the moral person which legitimately acquired it. This title of ownership, however, is held under the supreme authority of the Holy See which acts as the supreme administrator and dispenser of all ecclesiastical goods.[29] Hence not only the Church Universal and the Apostolic See may be the subjects of ownership, but also the individual institutions which the Church has established as juridical entities, and which are canonically referred to as inferior or subordinate moral persons.[30]

Section 1. The Collection of Alms and Taxes

The most common means, besides the contract of sale recognized and employed by the Church in acquiring temporal goods are: tithes, first-fruits, tributes, taxes, pious foundations, last wills, legacies, donations and prescription or adverse possession. Such means are in strict accord

[27] Cocchi, *Commentarium in Codicem Iuris Canonici ad Usum Scholarum* (8 vols., Vol. VI, 3. ed. Taurinorum Augustae: Marietti, 1933), VI, p. 348, n. 171 (hereafter cited as Cocchi).

[28] Can. 1499, § 1—Ecclesia acquirere bona temporalia potest omnibus iustis modis iuris sive naturalis sive positivi, quibus id aliis licet.

[29] Can. 1499, § 2—Dominium bonorum, sub suprema auctoritate Sedis Apostolicae, ad eam pertinet moralem personam, quae eadem bona legitime acquisiverit.

[30] Cocchi, VI, 351.

with justice, and are similar in many respects to the means whereby other corporations acquire property.[31]

The Church declares that the payment of tithes and first-fruits is a practice which is to be governed by the special laws and praiseworthy customs of each country.[32] At present there is no general law demanding such payment, but if there should be a special law or custom in some country requiring it, the Church decrees that it must be observed. Since there has never been such a provision in this country, the payment of tithes and first-fruits is not of practical consideration in this study.

The acquisition of temporal goods through the collection of alms and taxes is a practice as old as the Church itself. Such collections include offerings freely given by the faithful upon request or of their own motion, and offerings legitimately imposed upon them in the manner of a tax.[33] Regardless of how they are given, such offerings have as their purpose the support of the universal Church, or of some parish, mission, individual church or pious ecclesiastical cause.

To prevent abuses which have occurred through alms-collecting in the past, and properly to regulate this practice, the Church has imposed upon the clergy and laity the obligation of obtaining proper permission before attempting to collect alms by requesting them. This permission is required of those who act thus in a private capacity. The authorization must be obtained in writing either from the Holy See through the proper Congregation or from the local ordinary and the collector's own ordinary. If the collectors are religious persons (members of a religious community) it is further demanded that the provisions of canons 621-624 are to be observed.[34]

[31] Doheny, *Church Property*, p. 36.

[32] Can. 1502—Ad decimarum et primitiarum solutionem quod attinet, peculiaria statuta ac laudabiles consuetudines in unaquaque regione serventur.

[33] Vromant, *De Bonis Ecclesiae Temporalibus*, p. 97, n. 73.

[34] Cf. can. 1503—Salvis praescriptis can. 621-624, vetantur privati tam clerici quam laici sine Sedis Apostolicae aut proprii Ordinarii

Canons 1504-1507 determine the power of local ordinaries to impose taxes directly or indirectly upon the faithful. Among such taxes are the *cathedraticum* and those which are exacted in fulfillment of some special need arising in a diocese.

The *cathedraticum* is a moderate fee paid annually to a bishop as an expression of subjection.[35] It is not paid, therefore, as a means of supplying all of the necessary support for the bishop, but rather in continuance of the ancient practice of manifesting submission to the episcopal see, as a reminder that parish churches are dependent upon the cathedral church. The *cathedraticum* is classified as an ordinary tax inasmuch as it should be moderate or small and uniformly determined for all juridical persons paying it. The amount of the tribute is not to be decided according to the annual income of the churches or by the number of the faithful.[36] The Code does not determine the exact amount to be paid, but permits it to be decided by provincial councils or by a meeting of the bishops of the province, unless the amount has been established through a customary usage of long standing.[37]

Since the *cathedraticum* is to be given primarily in a spirit of submission and in honor of the episcopal see, it can be exacted only in the name of the bishop. According to a decree of the Sacred Congregation of the Council, therefore, it is not to be paid when the see is vacant, and it cannot be demanded by the Apostolic Administrator or any other person who rules the diocese during the vacancy.[38]

et Ordinarii loci licentia, in scriptis data, stipem cogere pro quolibet pio aut ecclesiastico instituto vel fine. Cf. also Doheny, *Church Property*, p. 51.

[35] Cocchi, VI, p. 360, n. 178. [36] *Loc. cit.*

[37] Can. 1504—Omnes ecclesiae vel beneficia iurisdictioni Episcopi subiecta, itemque laicorum confraternitates, debent quotannis in signum subiectionis solvere Episcopo cathedraticum seu moderatam taxam determinandam ad normam can. 1507, § 1, nisi iam antiqua consuetudine fuerit determinata.

[38] Cf. S.C.C., 13 mart. 1920—*AAS*, XII (1920), 445, 446.

Besides the *cathedraticum,*[39] the tax for the support of the seminary,[40] and the pensions imposed upon benefices in favor of retiring pastors,[41] the local ordinary may exact an extraordinary tax from all benefices, secular and religious, if he judges that the needs of the diocese demand it. This tax is known as the charitable subsidy.[42] The amount of this tax is not determined by law. It is left to the option of the bishop to judge what is needed for the good of the diocese. The tax, however, must remain an extraordinary and moderate one, and the bishop must have a just cause for imposing it.[43]

The local ordinary may also impose additional taxes on churches, benefices and ecclesiastical institutes for the benefit of the diocese or in favor of a patron, but he may do this only in connection with the act of foundation or consecration. He may not, however, impose any tax upon stipends for foundation Masses or upon ordinary Mass stipends.[44]

It is left to provincial councils or to other assemblies of the bishops of a province to determine the fees to be exacted for the various acts of voluntary jurisdiction, for the execution of papal rescripts, or upon the occasion of the ministration of the sacraments and sacramentals. In all of these instances, since certain benefits are conferred

[39] Can. 1504.

[40] Canons 1355, 1356.

[41] Can. 1429.

[42] Can. 1505—Loci Ordinarius, praeter tributum pro Seminario, de quo in can. 1355, 1356, aut beneficialem pensionem de qua in can. 1429, potest, speciali dioecesis necessitate impellente, omnibus beneficiariis, sive saecularibus sive religiosis, extraordinariam et moderatam exactionem imponere.

[43] Cf. Vermeersch-Creusen, *Epitome Iuris Canonici* (3 vols., Mechliniae-Romae: H. Dessain, Vol. II, 6. ed., 1940), II, p. 575, 576, n. 826 (hereafter cited as Vermeersch-Creusen).

[44] Can. 1506—Aliud tributum in bonum dioecesis vel pro patrono imponere ecclesiis, beneficiis aliisque institutis ecclesiasticis, quanquam sibi subiectis, Ordinarius potest tantummodo in actu fundationis vel consecrationis; sed nullum imponi tributum potest super eleemosynis Missarum sive manualium sive fundatarum.

upon individuals either through the reception of divine grace or otherwise, every danger of simony in violation of either the divine or the ecclesiastical law is to be avoided, according to the provisions of canon 730. The Church exercises the greatest care in this regard by requiring that the rates established are to be approved by the Holy See before they become effective.[45]

Canon 1234, however, permits the local ordinary to decide the amount of tax for funerals within the diocese if it has not already been determined; and canon 1056 allows only a small offering to be exacted on the occasion of granting matrimonial dispensations, the purpose of such a fee being to defray chancery expenses. Finally, the ruling of canon 1909 is to be observed regarding the fees collected for juridical services.

Section 2. Acquisition by "Praescriptio"

The present Code continues to recognize the legal device of *"praescriptio"* as a legitimate means of acquiring property and rights and of freeing oneself from obligations. In the greater part of the Church's legislation on *"praescriptio"* the enactments of the civil laws have been adopted and canonized except insofar as they would violate the provisions of canons 1509-1512.[46] It should be noted that *"praescriptio,"* as employed by canon law, includes the adverse possession, prescription and limitation of actions of the American Law.[47]

[45] Can. 1507, § 1—Salvo praescripto can. 1056 et can. 1234 praefinire taxas pro variis actibus iurisdictionis voluntariae vel pro exsecutione rescriptorum Sedis Apostolicae vel occasione ministrationis Sacramentorum vel Sacramentalium, in toto ecclesiastica provincia solvendas, est Concilii provincialis aut conventus Episcoporum provinciae; sed nulla vi praefinitio eiusmodi pollet, nisi prius a Sede Apostolica approbata fuerit.

[46] Can. 1508—Praescriptionem, tanquam acquirendi et se liberandi modum prout est in legislatione civili respectivae nationis, Ecclesia pro bonis ecclesiasticis recipit, salvo praescripto canonum qui sequuntur.

[47] Martin, *Adverse Possession, Prescription and Limitation of*

Every supreme legislator has the power of withholding or withdrawing objects from the ordinary course of prescriptive action. The Church, therefore, by positive enactment, exempts certain things from the operation of "*praescriptio*," some of which exemptions have reference to temporal goods.[48] Among such objects withdrawn from the potential operation of "*praescriptio*" are those things that are of divine law, whether natural or positive.[49] Thus an article secured by theft could not be gained by "*praescriptio*," because the divine law against theft is beyond the control of human agencies.[50]

The boundaries of provinces, dioceses, parishes, apostolic vicariates, apostolic prefectures, abbacies and prelacies *nullius* are non-prescriptable when these have been definitely determined. Likewise, all Mass stipends, all benefices obtained without a title, and the tax called the *cathedraticum* cannot be acquired by way of "*praescriptio*."[51]

Among those things over which the Church exercises special jurisdiction, but which it allows to be acquired by "*praescriptio*," are sacred objects provided that certain restrictions are observed. Blessed or consecrated things which belong to private individuals can be acquired through "*praescriptio*" by other persons, but they may not be directed to profane uses. If they have lost their blessing or consecration they may be freely acquired for profane but not for unbecoming uses.[52] Those sacred objects which are

Actions: The Canonical "Praescriptio," The Catholic University of America Canon Law Studies, n. 202 (Washington D.C.: The Catholic University of America Press, 1944), p. 164 (hereafter cited as Martin).

[48] Cf. Doheny, *Church Property*, p. 73.

[49] Can. 1509, 1°—Praescriptioni obnoxia non sunt quae sunt iuris divini sive naturalis sive positivi.

[50] Doheny, *Church Property*, p. 73.

[51] Can. 1509, 4°, 5°, 6°, 8°.

[52] Can. 1510, § 1—Res sacrae quae in dominio privatorum sunt, praescriptione acquiri a privatis personis possunt, quae tamen eas adhibere nequeunt ad profanos usus; si vero consecrationem vel benedictionem amiserint, libere acquiri possunt etiam ad usus profanos, non tamen sordidos.

not in the possession of private persons cannot be acquired by a private person through *"praescriptio."* They can, however, be acquired by one ecclesiastical corporation through *"praescriptio"* against another, whether these moral persons be collegiate or non-collegiate.[53]

The Code establishes a special period of time for the prescription of some of the Church's property. After a period of one hundred years it is permitted to claim by way of *"praescriptio"* those things which pertain to the Holy See and which are classified as immovable objects, as well as movable things that are precious.[54]

If these same articles belong to other church corporations, they pass by *"praescriptio"* after a lapse of thirty years.[55] It is evident, therefore, that canon 1511 makes a definite departure from the civil law enactments regarding the period of time required for *"praescriptio."* This would be particularly noticeable in this country where there is little uniformity in the legislation of the various states. The law of Ohio, with which this study is chiefly concerned, has set the period of time for the prescription of immovable objects at twenty-one years.[56]

Since the law of the Church exalts the human conscience by emphasizing the personal responsibility of individuals before God and the court of law, the Code insists upon the continuance of good faith during the entire period of *"praescriptio."*[57] This is another evidence of a difference between

[53] Can. 1510, § 2—Res sacrae, quae in dominio privatorum non sunt, non a persona private, sed a persona morali ecclesiastica contra aliam personam moralem ecclesiasticam praescribi possunt.

[54] Can. 1511, § —Res immobiles, mobiles pretiosae, iura et actiones sive personales sive reales, quae pertinent ad Sedem Apostolicam, spatio centum annorum praescribuntur.

[55] Can. 1511, § 2—Quae [pertinent] ad aliam personam moralem ecclesiasticam, spatio triginta annorum [praescribuntur].

[56] Bouvier, *Law Dictionary and Concise Encyclopedia,* II, 2671-2673.

[57] Can. 1512—Nulla valet praescriptio, nisi bona fide nitatur, non solum initio possessionis, sed toto possessionis tempore ad praescriptionem requisito.

canonical and civil legislation, inasmuch as the civil laws of most nations call for the actual existence of good faith only at the beginning of the lapsing period of prescription.[58] Under the present Code, if a person enters upon possession knowing that he is not entitled to such possession, he is unable to claim title later by adverse possession or prescription. If he enters upon possession with a serious doubt in his mind whether he is entitled to do so, he must clear up such doubt or he cannot later claim title by way of adverse possession. If during the period of the adverse possession he comes to the knowledge that he is not entitled to possession, the holder under the Code can no longer claim title by adverse possession. If a serious doubt as to his title arises during this period, then the holder must clear it up or in some way resolve it, else he cannot claim title by adverse possession.[59]

Section 3. Donations and Bequests

From the earliest centuries the Church has been the recipient of property through donations and last wills and testaments. It has always asserted its jurisdiction over such gifts and bequests when made in favor of religion or charity by persons having the right to dispose of their goods. If owners are not restricted by the natural or the ecclesiastical law, the Code vindicates their right to give or leave property to the Church as they desire.[60] Canon 583 affords an example of an ecclesiastical restriction regarding donations and last wills. It forbids members of religious communities in simple profession to give away or make a donation of their goods and to change the last will which they are required to make at the end of the novitiate, unless they have obtained permission from the Holy

[58] Doheny, *Church Property*, p. 79.

[59] Martin, pp. 53-54.

[60] Can. 1513, §—Qui ex iure naturae et ecclesiastico libere valet de suis bonis statuere, potest ad causas pias, sive per actum inter vivos sive per actum mortis causa, bona relinquere.

See or, in urgent cases, from the major or at least the local superior.[61]

As in the case of some of the canonical legislation on *"praescriptio,"* so also in regard to last wills and testaments there is now a strict obligation on the part of testators to observe the formalities required under the secular law for the validity of wills when they make bequests to charity and religion.[62] Two distinct obligations are involved in canon 1513, § 2. One rests on the testator, the other on the heir. The fact that the heir will be obliged to fulfill the will in any case does not excuse the testator from obeying the law as expressed in the canon.[63] The Church wishes to see the requirements of the civil law observed for reasons of convenience and security. This is a precautionary measure which when adopted facilitates and expedites the probation and filing of testamentary bequests. By thus conforming to the civil law requirements, however, the Church does not relinquish its rights to be beneficiary of wills and bequests, for no civil legislation could justly deprive the Church of property to which it has a strict right. If, therefore, a will were declared invalid by the civil law because of the omission of non-essential formalities, the Church could not admit such invalidity.[64] This is why the Code decrees that the formalities of civil law are to be observed if this is possible. If they are not observed, the heirs must nevertheless be warned of their obligation to fulfill the intentions of the testator irrespective of the civil provisions.[65]

[61] Professis a votis simplicibus in Congregationibus religiosis non licet: 1°. Per actum inter vivos dominium bonorum suorum titulo gratioso abdicare; 2°. Testamentum conditum ad normam can. 569, § 3, mutare sine licentia Sanctae Sedis, vel, si res urgeat nec tempus suppetat ad eam recurrendi, sine licentia Superioris maioris aut, si nec ille adiri possit, localis.

[62] Can. 1513, § 2—In ultimis voluntatibus in bonum Ecclesiae serventur, si fieri possit, sollemnitates iuris civilis; hae si omissae fuerint, heredes moneantur ut testatoris voluntatem adimpleant.

[63] Cf. Hannan, *The Canon Law of Wills*, pp. 283ff.

[64] Cf. Doheny, *Church Property*, pp. 89, 90.

[65] Can. 1513, § 2.

CHAPTER V

THE LAW OF OHIO REGARDING THE ACQUISITION AND TENURE OF CHURCH PROPERTY

ARTICLE I. THE PROVISIONS OF THE CONSTITUTION OF OHIO

The Constitution of the United States, in delimiting the legislative powers of Congress, has never granted to it the permission to enact any law recognizing the Church as a corporation that exists in its own right by divine institution, and that is capable of exercising civil rights irrespective of the government. Furthermore, to remove doubt or uncertainty from the minds of all citizens in this matter, the first amendment to the constitution was proposed and adopted. It provides that "Congress shall make no law respecting an establishment of religion or prohibiting the free exercise thereof." Section 2, Article IV, of the Federal Constitution provides that "citizens of each State shall be entitled to all of the privileges and immunities of citizens in the several States." This provision, however, has been held by the United States Supreme Court to have no reference to the question of religious liberty.[1] By the tenth amendment to the Constitution the individual States retained "all of the powers not delegated to the United States by the Constitution and not prohibited by it to the States." Therefore the whole power over the subject of religion is left exclusively to the state governments, to be acted upon according to their sense of justice and their constitutions. Any action taken by an individual State to establish a particular religion or to prohibit the free exercise of one or all religions would not be contrary to the Federal Constitution.[2]

[1] 16 Wallace, (U.S.) 36.

[2] Cf. Zollmann, *American Church Law* (St. Paul, Minn., West Publishing Co., 1933) p. 8, §§ 6, 7.

The State of Ohio, however, as well as the other States, has adopted the same view as the federal government in its attitude toward religion. It does not directly recognize or treat the Church as a corporate entity, but Ohio purports to grant to citizens, whether members of a religious society or not, a full measure of religious freedom within reasonable bounds. Article I, Section 7, of the Constitution of the State of Ohio declares:

> All men have a natural and indefeasible right to worship Almighty God according to the dictates of their own conscience. No person shall be compelled to attend, erect, or support any place of worship or maintain any form of worship against his consent; and no preference shall be given by law to any religious society; nor shall any interference with the rights of conscience be permitted. No religious test shall be required as a qualification for office nor shall any person be incompetent to be a witness on account of his religious belief; but nothing herein shall be construed to dispense with oaths and affirmations. Religion, morality, and knowledge, however, being essential to good government, it shall be the duty of the General Assembly to pass suitable laws to protect every religious denomination in the peaceable enjoyment of its own mode of public worship, and to encourage schools and the means of instruction.[3]

According to commentators and in keeping with decisions handed down by the Supreme Court of Ohio, this specification of the constitution "secures to every citizen of the State the fullest liberty of conscience in matters of religion. No one can be compelled to support or observe any form of worship against his consent. Accordingly, no interference with the rights of conscience is permitted. The constitution recognizes and guarantees unqualified liberty of religious faith. It is not by mere toleration that every individual is protected in his religious belief or disbelief. He reposes

[3] Baldwin, *Ohio Revised Code, Annotated: Certified Text of Laws as officially adopted* (Banks-Baldwin Company, Cleveland, 1953), p. 3 (hereafter cited as *Baldwin's Ohio Revised Code*).

not upon the leniency of government or the liberality of any class or sect of men, but upon his natural indefeasible rights of conscience which are beyond the control or interference of any human authority. Religion is eminently one of those interests lying outside the true and legitimate province of government. It is not within the purview of human government. Religion is essentially distinct from human government and exempt from its cognizance. A connection between them is injurious to both."[4]

Religious liberty in Ohio, however, as freely as it is granted and guaranteed by the courts in interpreting the constitution, is not without restriction. "It does not include the right to introduce and carry out every scheme or purpose which persons see fit to claim as a part of their religious system. It does not consist in the right of any sect to oppose its views to the policy of a government. Acts evil in their nature, or dangerous to the public welfare, may be forbidden and punished though sanctioned by one religion and prohibited by another. While laws cannot interfere with mere religious belief and opinions, they may with practices. The exercise of police power may occasionally qualify religious freedom."[5]

[4] *Ohio Jurisprudence: A Complete Statement of the Law and Practice of the State of Ohio* (43 vols., Vol. VIII, The Lawyers Cooperative Publishing Company, 1930) VIII, pp. 495-497, §§ 356-357 (hereafter cited as *Ohio Jur.*)
Bloom *v.* Richards (1853), 2 *Ohio State* 387: Neither Christianity nor any other system of religion is a part of the law of Ohio. The government has never been invested with authority to enforce any religious observance simply because it is religious. Therefore, a contract entered into on a Sunday was not, for that reason, void at common law.
Board of Education *v.* Minor (1872), 23 Ohio State, 211: The constitution of the state does not enjoin or require religious instruction or the reading of religious books in the public schools of the state.

[5] 8 *Ohio Jur.*, pp. 497, § 358.
Kisor *v.* Stancifer (1834), 6 *Ohio State*, 363: In a situation, however, where it was deemed necessary to make inquiries concerning the tenets of a body of worshippers for the purpose of settling a right of property dependent upon such tenets, the question was considered one of

The government of Ohio not only permits individuals to embrace religious beliefs and practices of their choice, but it also allows citizens to organize themselves into groups or societies for religious purposes. From the earliest days of the State's sovereign existence church or religious associations have been recognized and treated as bodies entitled to enjoy certain benefits, among which have been the benefits of property; and such property has been protected and secured to them by law.[6] To establish a religious society it is required that there be a definite membership of persons associated together, with or without officers. These persons collectively constitute the society. Under some systems each church or religious society is an independent body with a congregational form of government not subject to the control of any higher ecclesiastical body. Under other systems the local church is but a member of a larger religious organization and under its government and control.

A church or religious society may exist for all of the purposes for which it was organized, independently of any corporation of the body. It is a matter of common knowledge that many such societies do exist and are never incorporated. However, before a religious body can take the position of a contracting party, the members must organize, assume a name and choose from their number trustees. When they have done so, the body is said to stand in the law as one artificial person with the general rights and powers, and subject to the obligations and duties of a natural person. When it is thus organized by the legislature of Ohio, it is authorized and empowered to purchase, acquire, hold and convey real estate or personal property, make contracts, execute deeds, employ agents, sue and be sued, and be liable on its contracts and for its torts. Changes in the membership of congregations do not affect their

property rather than one of conscience, and was held not included in the constitutional inhibition.

[6] 35 *Ohio Jur.*, p. 335, § 25.

legal identity. They remain, in legal contemplation, the same congregations and bodies, continuing and enjoying the religious uses to which the properties possessed by them are devoted.[7]

To sum up the constitutional provisions regarding religion, it can be said that the citizens of Ohio are guaranteed religious freedom and that they are permitted to associate together as members of religious societies in the enjoyment of this liberty. All religious societies are equal before the law, but they are not recognized *ipso facto* as corporations having civil rights, although they can be chartered as corporations and thus can become artificial persons. Since the divinely granted personality of the Church is denied, the Church's freedom, particularly in property matters, is subject to definite restrictions. The Church may enjoy the benefits of property in Ohio, but its right to acquire, hold and administer such property is not admitted as a native right independent of the civil authority. Any capacity which the Church holds over property is granted by state authority which may likewise revoke it or restrict it. In general these restrictions are similar to those in all of the States. The Catholic Church as such is considered not a corporation but a hierarchy. Neither the Pope nor any bishop will be accorded any authority except a spiritual one. As an ecclesiastical system the Church, in this country, has neither legal capacity nor legal existence, and it is incapable *suo iure* of having legal rights or temporal property. The contention, therefore, that the Catholic Church as such may own property is called an inconceivable assumption. As a sovereign power it can acquire property in the various States only by treaty with the government at Washington.[8]

This attitude of state governments indicates that the rights of church members are emphasized rather than the rights of the Church itself. The primary concern of the

[7] 35 *Ohio Jur.*, pp. 309, 310, § 5.

[8] Cf. Zollmann, *American Church Law*, p. 112.

courts is not the spiritual society as such but the citizens within it, insofar as they possess rights to religious freedom under the State constitution. The States guarantee those rights in church property matters by permitting such property to be held by religious societies for the definite religious purposes specified. To understand how and to what extent the Church enjoys the benefits of property in Ohio, it will be necessary to examine the legislation of the State as it affects religious societies.

Article II. The Manner and Nature of the Tenure of Church Property

Section 1. The Incorporation of Religious Societies

The history of legislation in Ohio reveals that the Catholic Church and other religious societies have been permitted to acquire and hold property just as private individuals. They have even been capable of taking both personal property and real estate by devise.[9] Since the law, however, does not recognize the personality of religious societies as such, they may hold property only in the manner which the statutes permit.

Under the Ohio law there exist both religious corporations and unincorporated religious societies. The title to property, therefore, is acquired, held and administered in different ways.

An incorporating statute of the State's Code makes the following provision:

When a diocesan convention or other representa-

[9] Cf. 35 *Ohio Jur.*, p. 335, § 25.
American Bible Soc. *v.* Marshall (1864), 15 *Ohio State*, 537: Where the terms of the charter of a corporation created by the legislation of another state are sufficiently broad to confer upon it a capacity to take and hold real estate by devise, although not *expressly* authorized so to take, a provision of the statute of wills of that state that "no devise of real estate to a corporation shall be valid unless such corporation be expressly authorized by its charter or by statute to take by devise," is operative only to the extent of disabling the corporation to take by devise real estate situated in that state, and does not affect its power to take by devise real estate in Ohio.

> tive body of any religious denomination in this state desires the incorporation of a Cathedral or other central or general religious society or church of its denomination, having, in addition to local religious, educational, or charitable functions, a general charge of such functions and of missionary functions in the diocese or other ecclesiastical territory in this state represented by said body, and when at any regular meeting of such representative body it elects not less than five members of such denomination, at least one of whom is a resident freeholder in this state, to serve as members of the chapter or trustees of the society being incorporated until the election of their successors, and makes a statement giving the names of such members or trustees, the character of the endowment fund or other property, donations or appropriations to be entrusted to their care and the uses to which such fund, property, donations and appropriations are to be applied, the general rights, powers and duties of such members or trustees, and the corporate name by which they are to be known, which statement is signed, certified, attested, acknowledged, filed and recorded in the office of the secretary of the state in the manner prescribed by section 1715.12 of the Revised Code for statements filed under such section, then the members or trustees, so named thereupon, with their successors in office, under such corporate name, become a body corporate and politic for the purpose specified in such statement. A copy of such record, certified by the secretary of state, shall be evidence of the existence of such corporation.[10]

When a religious society incorporates under this statute it becomes subject to the laws governing corporations not for profit. Such corporations may "acquire, hold, convey, lease, mortgage, or dispose of all property, real or personal, which is necessary or expedient to accomplish their pur-

[10] Page, *Page's Ohio Revised Code, Annotated* (Cincinnati, Ohio: W. H. Anderson Co., 1954), Title 17, § 1715.18 (hereafter cited as *Page's Ohio Revised Code*).

poses.[11] It is stated further that "all property, real or personal, acquired by a corporation not for profit by purchase, gift, or otherwise, shall be the absolute property of such corporation unless at the time of acquiring such property it is otherwise in writing specified."[12] If the Church, therefore, wishes to resort to corporate devices for the purpose of acquiring and holding property, it may do so by becoming a private corporation. When this is done the Church is said to consist of two elements: first, the ecclesiastical body, which undergoes no change by the fact of incorporation; and secondly, the corporation itself, a creature of the law, which has relation only to the temporalities of the institution. In such a case it is not the Church as a spiritual society, but the corporation as a person in private law, that holds the property. It is with the corporation as a private entity, and not with the Church as such, that the civil law deals in matters affecting church property.[13]

In holding property by means of a corporate capacity the Church itself and the corporation are always looked upon and treated as being absolutely distinct. They are derived from different sources and they have different powers. The fact that each individual may stand in the dual capacity of a member of the corporation and a member of the Church does not alter the situation. Although the corporation exists within the pale of the Church and vice versa, the two bodies are in no way considered correlative. The corporation has no spiritual capacity or denominational character. It is not ecclesiastical in its functions and has nothing to do with the Church except according as it provides for its wants. It is a subordinate factor in the life and purposes of the Church, having no concern with church work proper. It is not created to preach or to administer the Sacraments. It is a mere business agent with the sole purpose of making contracts and of acquiring,

[11] Page, *Page's Ohio General Code, Annotated* (Cincinnati: W. H. Anderson Company, 1938), § 8623-99.

[12] *Page's Ohio Revised Code,* Tit. 17, § 1702-19.

[13] Bartlett, *Tenure of Parochial Property,* p. 31.

holding, managing and disposing of property. It is a purely secular agency, a humble handmaid of the Church, created by the State to conduct the business affairs of the Church. The sole effect which it has on the State is simply to add another private corporation to the great number of such bodies.

Although the aims or purposes of religious corporations are different from those of other classes of corporations, they have no higher status than other societies organized by citizens. Since they are created for the purpose of managing church property, they are endowed with substantially the same rights and are subject to substantially the same liabilities and governed by substantially the same rules as are other private corporations. They are equal to natural persons so far as real estate and trusts are concerned. Insofar as the they have authority to make contracts they are subject to the ordinary rules of law and equity applicable to any other contracting party. Religious organizations come before the courts in the same manner as other voluntary associations for benevolent or charitable purposes, and their rights of property or of contract are equally under the protection of the law, and the actions of their members subject to its restraint. They are subject, therefore, to visitation, the requirement of reports, taxation based on their right of existence, the requirement for filing inventories, lists of practices, usages and laws. They are also subject to execution or termination of their corporate existence.[14]

Section 2. Church Property Held in Trust

In Ohio, at the present time, charitable and benevolent institutions under the ownership, control and management of religious communities belonging to the Catholic Church are separately incorporated and therefore hold their property in that manner. Although the Catholic dioceses may incorporate under the statute quoted above, *de facto* they

[14] Cf. Zollmann, *American Church Law*, pp. 132-133, 145-146, 151.

are unincorporated and as such they are without capacity to acquire or hold title to property. These unincorporated societies enjoy the benefits of property by means of trust tenure. They are permitted to constitute, by deed, trustees for the purpose of acquiring and holding property to be devoted to some particular use, usually for the purposes consistent with their creation and existence.[15] The General Code of Ohio provides that "lands not exceeding twenty acres that have been, or may be, conveyed by devise, purchase, or otherwise to any person or persons in trust for the use of a religious society, either for a meeting house, burying ground or parsonage, shall descend with the improvements and appurtenances in perpetual succession in trust to such trustees as from time to time are elected or appointed by such society, according to its rules, customs, usages and regulations."[16] Property conveyed in trust for the use of a religious society, church or association, whether incorporated or not, shall be held by the trustee or trustees, so appointed, and their successors, appointed as provided in the instrument creating the trust, or in case no provision is made in such instrument, then by such successor or successors as are appointed by such society, church or association, to act as trustees, to the exclusion of any trustee or trustees appointed as aforesaid."[17] The properly qualified members of a religious society, therefore, have the right to use and enjoy its property in conformity with the terms of the trust under which it is held, the rules of the society, and the regulations enacted by the trustees or other governing body.[18]

[15] Cf. 35 *Ohio Jur.*, p. 337, § 27.

[16] *Page's Ohio General Code*, § 10,020.

Morgan *v.* Leslie: Wright (Ohio) 144: It was held that the limitation of twenty acres referred not to a large denomination in Ohio, but to each individual church.

[17] *Page's Ohio General Code*, § 10,022.

[18] 35 *Ohio Jur.*, p. 342, § 31.

Mannix *v.* Purcell (1888), 46 *Ohio State*, 102: It is not essential to the existence or enjoyment of a trust for charitable uses that the individual beneficiaries are able to show that they contributed to,

To determine in whom, precisely, the title to property vests under Ohio's trust tenure, the courts look first to the terms of the instrument conveying the property to the society. When the instrument is silent on the matter, or when its terms are obscure, the customs, traditions and laws of the society may also be considered.[19] Since the title, however, is not held absolutely by the trustees or by the beneficiaries, it is important to understand the nature of a trust and the manner in which it operates to secure property for the benefit of the Church.

The courts of Ohio, in the exercise of their jurisprudence, have described and defined trusts. They have regarded them with favor and have sought grounds to support them. A trust is described as a creature of equity. It arises where the title to property is conferred upon, and accepted by, one person on the terms of holding, using, or disposing of it for the benefit of another. A trust is in the nature of the disposition by which a proprietor transfers to another property with which he is to be intrusted; not that it should remain with him but that it should be applied to certain uses in behalf of another. A trust is the right, enforceable in equity, to the beneficial enjoyment of property, the legal title of which is in another. The person who creates the trust is said to settle it on another and bears such designations as 'donor,' 'settlor,' or 'trustor.' He to whom the title to property is given in trust and in whom the legal title vests, is named the trustee. The person for whose benefit the trust is created is called the *cestui que trust*, or beneficiary. The property given in trust is called the subject

or have a personal pecuniary interest in, the trust property. Their interest is measured by, and limited to, the uses for which the property is held. Cf. Syllabus. (The syllabus is always found at the beginning of the report of each case).

[19] 35 *Ohio Jur.*, p. 338, § 27.

Mannix *v.* Purcell (1888), 46 *Ohio State*, 102: The canons and decrees of the Roman Catholic Church regulating the mode of acquiring and holding church property are competent evidence to show that property deeded to an archbishop individually is held by him in trust for religious and charitable societies. Cf. Syllabus.

matter, or *trust res.* The basic idea of a trust is this separate coexistence of the legal title with the beneficial ownership or, as it came to be called, the equitable title. The perfect or absolute ownership is said to be decomposed into its constituent elements of legal title and beneficial interests, which are vested in different persons at the same time. In the creation of trusts, therefore, there is a splitting of interests.[20]

Three factors are always necessary for every trust relationship. They are: (1) the person who creates the trust and who is called the settlor; (2) suitable subject matter, i.e., a *trust res* or property, and (3) the person or persons for whom the property is being held and in whose favor the trust purpose is to operate, i.e., the *cestui que trust* or beneficiary. The relationship which arises in the creation of the trust is called fiduciary inasmuch as one party trusts his property or interest to the dominion of another and relies upon the integrity of that other party to do nothing that would impair the interests confided in him.[21] In the early history of equity and trusts, the performance of the trust was left entirely with the conscience of the trustee. In Ohio, however, the trust is not valid unless it is enforceable in the court. "The law knows no trust which simply binds the conscience. An alleged trust which is cognizable only in the court of morals or the forum of conscience is no trust at all: it is an absurdity. The law does not acknowledge a trust over the exercise of which it will not, through its tribunals, assume control to avert its destruction, perversion or abuse."[22] Courts of equity, therefore, will not create trusts, since it is not within their power to establish fiduciary relationships, but the courts will uphold and enforce a trust if there is adequate proof that it exists. It is consequently important that trusts be created with proper care, for it must be proved that such trusts have been expressly or implicitly established.

[20] 40 *Ohio Jur.*, pp. 96-98.
[21] 40 *Ohio Jur.*, pp. 96-97.
[22] Mannix *v.* Purcell (1888), 46 *Ohio State*, 102.

An express trust must be created by the settlor. If he is *sui iuris* he may create an express trust by an *inter vivos* declaration, deed, or enforceable agreement or by a testamentary disposition, or by an effective creation of an imperative power.[23]

If an owner of property who is *sui iuris* wishes to declare that he holds such property in trust for another, he may do so either orally or in writing. The declaration must be a completely executed transaction complying with the requirements of consideration, and it will thus have the effect of creating a trust immediately. The intention to become a trustee must be clearly expressed.[24]

It is impossible to have a trust without a *trust res.* A trust must always be created with respect to property. Anything which has economic or exchange value is usually proper subject matter for the creation of a trust. It must, however, be transferable, in actual existence, and ascertainable at the time of the creation of the trust. Real or tangible personal property furnishes the subject matter for almost all trusts, but there can be included also such intangible property as life insurance policies, a cause of action, patent rights, copyrights, trademarks, equitable interests, an imperative power, etc.[25]

The trustee is required to take an estate or interest in the *trust res* sufficient in extent to enable him to exercise the powers and duties imposed upon him in the administration of the trust. The settlor's intention is controlling in this respect. Usually in the deed or will an estate or title is conveyed or transferred to the trustee. If the instrument creating the trust confers upon the trustee mandatory powers but fails to transfer any estate to him, there will be implied an estate sufficient to enable the trustee to

[23] 40 *Ohio Jur.*, p. 140.
Faurot *v.* Neff (1876), 32 *Ohio State*, 44: An express trust is raised and created by the act, consent and mutual understanding of the parties. Cf. Syllabus.

[24] 40 *Ohio Jur.*, pp. 141-142.

[25] *Ibid.*, pp. 186-189.

carry out the powers given.[26] Hence two qualifications are usually necessary in any trustee. He must have the capacity to receive and hold the title to property, real or personal, and he must have business capacity to carry on the management of the trust.

The trust instrument may be little more than an instrument of transfer, passing the title of the property to the trustee with a declaration of the trust purpose. In such a case, practically all of the powers and duties which the trustee may exercise or be required to assume are those imposed upon him by the court of equity or by the general statute. If the power given in the instrument creating the trust leaves the exercise of such powers with the discretion of the trustee, the power is characterized as mere naked power. If the power is made imperative and not personal, then it is said to be a power in trust, and the failure of the trustee to exercise such a power will not be fatal to it, but a successor will be appointed to execute the same.[27]

Further rules binding trustees will be considered in a later chapter of this study, where the question of the administration of church property will be treated. The chief concern here is to understand the essential elements and operations involved in the creation of trusts, especially insofar as they are upheld by the courts of Ohio in favor of religious societies. It is peculiarly within the province of a court of equity to enforce trusts, including donations of property and funds for general or specific religious purposes. Where a trust is created in such a manner as to give to the trustees of a religious society the discretion of naming the beneficiaries, or where the terms of the trust are not so definite as to designate all those who are entitled to its benefit, much is left to the judgment of the trustees, and when it is exercised in good faith equity will not interfere.[28] Where it is not shown that the trustees of

[26] *Ibid.*, pp. 192-194.
[27] *Ibid.*, pp. 332-333.
[28] 35 *Ohio Jur.*, p 356, § 44.

a religious or charitable fund have wilfully misapplied the funds of the trust, but rather have displayed a deplorably lax method in the management of the society, the court will endeavor to effect a reorganization of the management and business methods without appointing a receiver therefor.[29]

As a general rule, therefore, it may be said that a trust for public worship and other charitable purposes is one of which the laws of Ohio will take cognizance and assume control, exercising its authority in seeing that the property is applied to the uses for which it was acquired, and not to inconsistent purposes. Thus, if property is donated for the express purpose of being held and exclusively used for the teaching, support, or maintenance of some specific dogma, creed or form of religion declared by the instrument under which the property is held, a trust arises, and a court of equity will prevent a diversion of the trust attached to the use so long as there are persons or agencies within the meaning of the original dedication who are willing to carry out the intended uses.

The courts of Ohio have thus indicated that the first impulse of the legal mind, with respect to trusts for religious purposes, is to regard them favorably and to seek grounds for supporting them. This has been amply demonstrated by the decision handed down in the leading case, Mannix *v.* Purcell (1888).[30] The Supreme Court of Ohio not only defined the nature of a religious trust but also ruled that such a trust existed even where the grant of title to property was absolute. Inasmuch as the decision affected, and still affects, the security of church property, the case should be given careful examination.

John B. Purcell was appointed Bishop of the Diocese of Cincinnati in 1833. When the diocese was elevated to the rank of an archdiocese in 1859, he remained as its ordinary. During the course of his long tenure of office he

[29] *Loc. cit.*

[30] 46 *Ohio State*, 102.

appointed his brother, Father Edward Purcell, as Vicar General. Among other duties Father Purcell was placed in charge of the financial business of the diocese. In consequence of the financial panic which occurred in 1837, many individuals became distrustful of the banks and they deposited their savings with the ordinary who, through his brother, received the money on deposit and loaned it out upon interest. This activity continued for about forty years until the indebtedness incurred amounted to more than $3,800,000. During a period of depression in 1878, many of the Archbishop's creditors sought the return of their money, and it was found that he was unable to cover the deposits with their accumulated interest, since he had lost great sums in bank failures and through individuals who were indebted to him. Archbishop Purcell met this situation by assuming the debt as his own and, in his individual capacity, he made an assignment in insolvency of all of his property which could at law or in equity be subjected to such payment, excluding, however, all property held by him in trust for others.[31]

At that time the canons and decrees of the Church, as they affected the Archdiocese of Cincinnati, required that all ecclesiastical property was to be conveyed to the Archbishop in his own name, and to his heirs and assigns forever. In obedience to the Church's law, therefore, the churches, schools, orphan asylum, seminary and cemeteries were acquired and conveyed to the Archbishop in fee simple. Although the title on its face was absolute, the implication was that the Archbishop held the property in trust for ecclesiastical uses. Since there was overwhelming proof that a resulting trust actually existed, it seemed very likely that the indebtedness of the Archbishop would be charged to the trust, and thus the creditors would be legally unable to recover payment through his deed of assignment.[32]

[31] Cf. Lamott, *History of the Archdiocese of Cincinnati* (New York: Frederick Pustet Co., 1921), pp. 189-191.

[32] *Loc. cit.*

The creditors filed a petition to procure sale of the property, contending that the debts were those of the Archbishop individually, and that he was so far the absolute owner of the church property that the deed of assignment conveyed the property to the assignee. It was argued that no trust could attach to the church property of the diocese to defeat creditors and, furthermore, that the rules and canons of the Catholic Church were not admissible in evidence to establish, limit and define the trust.[33]

In contending that the debt was not a debt of the trust, the counsel for the churches and institutions proved that express trusts could be shown in some cases. It was admitted that it would be an innovation in the legal history of the United States if the court accepted the canons and decrees of the Catholic Church as evidence to establish the trust relationship of the Archbishop to the individual parish congregations. If, however, this evidence were ruled out, there remained the recourse to parol evidence to prove the existence of the trust. Such use of parol evidence was established beyond all doubt in the legal history of the State of Ohio.[34]

The Supreme Court of Ohio handed down its decision on December 21, 1888, in favor of the congregations and institutions by refusing to allow the diocesan property to be taken for the individual debts of Archbishop Purcell. The Court accepted the canons and decrees of the Church as evidence in the case, and in regard to the admission of parol evidence the following comment was made: "That parol evidence may be resorted to in order to engaft a trust upon a title held by deed absolute on its face is a question which in this State has passed beyond the range of serious discussion; though the proof in such cases should be clear, strong and convincing."[35]

[33] Mannix *v.* Purcell (1888), 46 *Ohio State* 102.

[34] Dignan, p. 221.

[35] Mannix *v.* Purcell at 136.

Mathews *v.* Leaman (1874) 24 *Ohio State* 615: In this state, notwithstanding the statute of frauds, it is competent to establish, by parol

In regard to accepting the law of the Church as evidence, the Court declared that "it is no innovation upon the law of evidence, in determining questions like the one at bar, to call, in aid of the civil tribunal, upon the law of the particular church involved for the purpose of determining the title to church property.... It is but a form of establishing, by convenient and very convincing proof, what entered into the contemplation of the parties to the grant at the time the title vested. It has been held that where a religious body becomes divided, and the right to the property is in conflict, the civil courts will consider and determine which of the divisions submits to the Church, local and general. This division is entitled to the property. In determining which of the divisions has maintained the correct doctrine, the findings of the supreme ecclesiastical tribunal of the denomination in question is binding upon the courts."[36]

It was also alleged in the case that the purposes to which the church property was devoted, as well as the beneficiaries, were all too indefinite for the trust to be upheld. In response to these allegations the Court stated that "the

evidence, that a deed of conveyance, absolute in form, was executed upon the consideration that the property conveyed was to be held in trust for the grantor, and reconveyed on demand. Cf. Syllabus.
Broadrup *v.* Woodman (1875) 27 *Ohio State* 553: A deed, absolute in form, by which land was conveyed was proved to be a deed of trust by the same evidence which the party had produced in a former suit relating to the same land and deed. Cf. Syllabus.

[36] Mannix *v.* Purcell at 137.
First Presbyterian Society *v.* Langley (1874), 25 *Ohio State* 128: Where a trust is created for the benefit of an incorporated religious society, and there are two bodies, each claiming to be such society, a court of equity may require the claimants to interplead, and may proceed to ascertain the true beneficiary without compelling either party to establish its corporate rights at law. Cf. Syllabus.
Price *et al. v.* Methodist Church *et al.* (1831), 4 *Ohio Reports* 515: Lands conveyed to trustees of the M.E. Church for the use of that Church according to its rules and discipline: the trustees cannot create any individual or public right inconsistent with the use prescribed by the discipline. Cf. Syllabus.

Cathedral and other church buildings have been . . . actually and openly possessed and used by their respective priests and congregations; the schools by their pupils and teachers; the orphan asylum by the Sisters of Charity in charge, and about four hundred orphans; and the graveyards by those in charge who have daily devoted them to the burial of the dead. . . . It has been said that vagueness is, in some respects, essential to a good gift to a public charity, and that a public charity begins where uncertainty in the recipient begins. . . . The individual recipients of the charity are constantly changing . . . yet it is in legal contemplation the same group."[37] The Court continued to say that the uses for which the property was dedicated were such as would be upheld; for since the Court had previously declared other trusts of a similar nature valid, and since those trusts were all sufficiently succinct in their objects, so then must be the uses, actual and contemplated by the canons of the Church.[38]

Counsel for the creditors also argued that the congregations and institutions, as beneficiaries, did not benefit by the uses attached to the property as they should if a real trust existed. They contended that if the ordinary actually held the property passively or upon resulting trust, the beneficiaries would have a right to demand that he convey

[37] Mannix *v.* Purcell at 140.

[38] Mannix *v.* Purcell at 142; Williams *v.* First Presbyterian Society (1853), 1 *Ohio State* 478. Other trust which the Court had previously declared valid were trusts for the education of youth; for the care, education and nurture of orphans; for the religious instruction of the living and the decent repose of the dead—Gerke *v.* Purcell (1874), 25 *Ohio State* 229; for the "use and support of a poor school which they are to establish for the use of the poor children of Zanesville"—McIntyre *v.* City of Zanesville (1867), 17 *Ohio State* 352; for the advancement and benefit of the Christian religion, to be applied in such a manner as in his judgment will best promote the object named—Miller *v.* Teachout (1874), 24 *Ohio State* 525; to the poor and needy, fatherless, etc., of Jefferson and Madison townships—Urmy *v.* Wooden (1853), 1 *Ohio State* 160; Sowers *v.* Syremus (1883), 39 *Ohio State* 29; Trustees *v.* Zanesville Canal Co. (1834), 9 *Ohio State* 203.

the legal title to them upon request. Since this request was never made, and since no conveyance took place, the alleged trust did not exist, and thus the full title vested in the Archbishop. The Court, however, found that the beneficiaries were consistently enjoying the uses attached to the property. Divine worship was being held regularly in the churches; classes were conducted daily in the schools, care was constantly given to orphans, and the cemeteries were open daily to receive the bodies of the deceased. Regarding the degree of property control vesting in the beneficiaries, the Court stated that "instead of asking that the head of the Church of the diocese convey, or be divested of, the legal title, the beneficiaries ask that it remain in him upon the same trusts and for the same uses to which, from the first, it had been devoted. Indeed, it is quite indispensable to the existence of the trust that the legal title be held by someone other than the *cestuis qui trustent* who are incapable, by reason of the indefiniteness which characterizes their personality, of holding it."[39] The Court, therefore, found no fault with a trust of such a nature that full authority vested in the trustee as indicated by the canons of the Church. It was inescapable that the tenure of the property demanded centralized control and power of disposal in the Archbishop. Since the parties involved in the trust relationship were in agreement concerning this kind of control, the trust was upheld and supported as valid under the laws of Ohio.[40]

ARTICLE III. ACQUISITION OF PROPERTY THROUGH GIFTS TO THE CHURCH AS A PUBLIC CHARITY

Section 1. The Legal Concept of Charitable Purposes and Gifts

It has been explained that unincorporated societies as such are without capacity to acquire and hold title to property in Ohio. Conveyances to these societies are therefore

[39] **Mannix *v.* Purcell at 145.**
[40] ***Loc. cit.***

void at law, but it is significant that courts of equity have been solicitous to uphold and preserve conveyances made to unincorporated religious associations. In such cases many of the courts have gone to great lengths in doing so. They have regarded the inability of unincorporated religious societies to take property at common law to be of little importance. The reason for this liberality is founded in the fact that religious purposes in Ohio and in the other States are recognized as important charitable purposes. They are placed in the same category as eleemosynary and educational charities, though they are distinct from these other recognized charities inasmuch as religious activities are not under state control. Religious charities nevertheless are regarded favorably in law, and gifts of property conveyed to them are upheld as gifts for the support of public charities. The law therefore gives recognition to the great value of religion in forming the characters of individual citizens and thereby promoting the general welfare of society. By acknowledging the validity of gifts for religious purposes the State fosters and encourages the free exercise of religion as guarantueed by its constitutional provisions.[41]

For a clearer understanding of how the Church is regarded as a public charity in Ohio, and to what extent it may thereby enjoy the benefits of property conveyed to it in the manner of gifts, it will be helpful to examine the notion of public charities and the nature of gifts to public charities as conceived and adopted by Ohio jurisprudence.

Charity, in its legal sense, is a thing to be described rather than defined. The meaning which charity ordinarily bears is different from its legal signification. Charity is not just aid to the needy, but it embraces all that aids man and improves his condition. It includes not only gifts for the poor, but also endowments for the advancement of learning, the encouragement of institutions of science and

[41] Zollman, *American Law of Charities* (Milwaukee, Bruce Publishing Co., 1924), pp. 161-164.

art, and for all useful public purposes without any particular reference to the poor.[42] When such useful public purposes have been constituted as charities, the law authorizes gifts of property for the benefit of these charitable purposes. Aid from individuals is thereby obtained to supply those wants and needs for which the State is obligated to provide. This is a function of government in the interest of society.[43]

For a charity to be valid, it must be public. In Ohio decisions it has often been necessary for the courts to determine the meaning of the terms in the phrases, "institutions of purely public charity," or "institutions used exclusively for charitable purposes," in interpreting the provisions of the constitution and the statutes. In the case, *Humphries v. Little Sisters of the Poor,* the Supreme Court ruled that a corporation created for the sole purpose of affording "an asylum for destitute men and women and the incurable sick and blind, irrespective of their nationality or creed," was an institution of purely public charity within the meaning of sec. 2, art. 12, of the constitution, and of sec. 3 of the tax law of 1859, which provided for the exemption of the property, therein described, from taxation. The Court also stated that the word "institutions," in the sixth clause of sec. 3 of the tax law, was used to designate the corporation or other organized body instituted to administer the charity, and that the real estate described as belonging to such institutions had reference to property owned by them; and to entitle such institutions to hold the property exempt from taxation, the Court required that they must not only own it, but that it must also be used in such a manner as to fulfill the requirements of the statute.[44]

The word "public" is used in various senses, sometimes to describe the use to which the property is devoted, and at other times to describe the manner in which it is held.

[42] 7 *Ohio Jur.*, pp. 112-113, § 2; Gerke *v.* Purcell (1874), 25 *Ohio State*, 229.

[43] Cf. Zollman, *American Law of Charities*, p. 120.

[44] Cf. Syllabus to 29 *Ohio State* 201.

In the case, *Gerke v. Purcell* (1874), it was held that the word "public," as applied to schoolhouses, was used to describe the ownership of the property, and that by "public school houses" was meant such as belonged to the public and were designed for schools established and conducted under public authority. The Court further stated that schools which were established by private donations and which were carried on for the benefit of the public, and not with a view to profit, were "institutions of purely public charity" within the meaning of the provision of the constitution, which authorized such institutions to be exempt from taxation. It was declared that the fact that the use of the property was free was not a necessary element in determining whether the use was public or not. If the use was of such a nature that it concerned the public, and if the right to its enjoyment was open to the public upon equal terms, the use was public, whether compensation was exacted or not.[45]

There are two kinds of public charities recognized by the law. One group is classified as public in the widest sense of that term, inasmuch as they are owned by the State for governmental purposes and maintained at public expense. Such institutions are absolutely under the control and management of the public through representatives, and thus no vested or private rights accrue from their erection and operation. The other group comprises those charities whose gifts of property are obtained by private donations. They are not subjected to absolute governmental control, since the organized public contributes nothing to them. The charity, however, which they administer is called a "public charity" in legal terminology.[46] The law permits gifts of real or personal property to be donated to these public charities, either *inter vivos* or by last will and testament. Realty may also be dedicated to public charitable use, and a trust in property may be declared in Ohio if it is done in clear and distinct terms, although its ultimate

[45] Syllabus to 25 *Ohio State* 229.

[46] Cf. 7 *Ohio Jur.*, pp. 113-118, § 3.

distribution may not be made until after the death of the donor. Whether a gift, however, is *inter vivos,* or *mortis causa,* or made through the medium of a trust, it is subject to the conditions imposed upon gifts by the law.[47]

Ohio jurists have defined a gift as a voluntary transfer of property by one to another without any consideration or compensation therefor. It is essential that the transfer of the subject matter of a gift be voluntary and without valuable consideration. The presence of compensation destroys the transaction as a gift, and the title therefore passes by purchase—not by deed of gift. The parties by their deed impress upon the title the character which it is to bear in the hands of the grantee and those who succeed him. If the grantors state only that the consideration is "good," they thereby impress upon the title the character of a deed of gift. If they state that the consideration is a "valuable" one, they thereby impress upon the title the character of title by purchase.[48]

Any person who is capable of holding title to property may be the recipient of a gift. Certain requirements, however, must be fulfilled for the validity of a gift. On the part of the donee, if he claims that property has been given to him by way of trust, it is necessary for him, as the beneficiary, to prove that an express and certain trust exists for his benefit. Though no particular form is necessary for its creation, the words or acts employed for establishing the trust should plainly imply that the party creating the trust intended to divest himself of his interest in the property and desired that it be held for the interest and benefit of another. On the part of the settlor, it is required that he either transfer the property to a trustee or declare that he himself holds it in trust. His acts must be of such a character that they will admit of only one interpretation, namely, that the legal rights which he retains, as settlor, are held by him as trustee for the donee. A mere intention to give

[47] *Ibid.* p. 122, § 5.
[48] 20 *Ohio Jur.*, pp. 4-5, § 2.

is not sufficient. The intended gift will fail unless its delivery is proved to be distinct and absolute. The donor, however, is not required to express his motive for his act of donation. His reasons for creating a trust on certain terms and conditions cannot be questioned by the courts. The true test of a gift to a legal public charity is the object sought—not the motive of the donor.[49]

Section 2. The Church as Beneficiary

The power to dispose of property by will in Ohio is conferred solely by statute, but not without some limitation or restriction. Although provision is made for the gift and bequest of any property, real or personal, to be lawfully executed, the owner of the property is not given a free hand in the disposition of his holdings. The statutes make the following provision:

> If a testator dies, leaving issue of his body or an adopted child living, or the legal representative of either, and the will of such testator gives, devises, or bequeaths the estate of such testator, or any part thereof, to a benevolent, religious, educational, or charitable purpose, or to this state or any other state or country, or to a county, city, village, or other corporation or association in this or any other state or country, or to a person in trust for such purposes, or municipalities, corporations or associations, whether such trust appears on the face of the instrument making such gift, devise or bequest or not; such will as to such gift, devise, or bequest, shall be invalid unless it was executed according to law at least one year prior to the death of the testator.[50]

According to civil law commentators, it was not intended by this provision to make the act of giving, devising or bequeathing property illegal; for the gift, devise or bequest which was declared to be invalid if the testator should die within one year from the execution of his will, may become valid by the lapse of time. It is therefore explained that

[49] Cf. 7 *Ohio Jur., op. cit.*, pp. 122-124.
[50] *Page's Ohio General Code,* § 10,504.

the limitation upon the testator's power of disposition is for the protection of the heir against improvident wills or those made under undue influence. We see, however, in the restriction of this statute, a vestige of the mortmain statutes; and although the statute is not discriminatory, nevertheless it is more rigorous than the natural divine law or the positive divine law, and thus it cannot be justly imposed.[51]

With the exception of this restriction, gifts to religious corporations have always been favored in the law of Ohio and, as was mentioned above, unincorporated religious societies have also been permitted to enjoy the benefits of property donated to them. In cases where gifts were given to other public charities the courts have required that they incorporate to have, thereby, the capacity of acquiring full title to the gift of property and thus to perpetuate and protect it. In cases, however, of gifts to religious charities, incorporation has not been required.[52] Whether they were incorporated or not, it has never been the policy to prohibit devises and bequests to religious societies. As early as 1825 an act was passed "securing to religious societies a perpetuity of title to lands and tenements conveyed in trust for meeting houses, burying grounds, or residence for preachers," and it provided that "such land that had been, or might be, conveyed to any person in trust for the use of any religious society should descend in perpetual succession to such trustees as should from time to time be appointed by any such religious society, according to its rules." This act was intended to remove all difficulties arising from defective conveyances, and it was held to be amply sufficient to effect the purpose of the trust, whether it was secret and implied, or expressed in the conveyance.[53]

This same act remained in force after the adoption of

[51] Cf. Abbo-Hannan, *The Sacred Canons* (2 vols., St. Louis, London: B. Herder Book Co., 1952), II, 710, footnote n. 2 (hereafter cited as Abbo-Hannan).

[52] Cf. 7 *Ohio Jur.*, pp. 132-133.

[53] *Ibid.*, p. 124.

the constitution in 1851, and there has not been discovered any intention to alter the law as it stood at that time.[54]

Gifts for the teaching, advancement and spread of Christianity, or for the convenience and support of worship, or for the ministry, have generally been held to be charitable. The fact that a gift is made to a particular religious denomination does not deprive it of its character as a public charity, and does not eliminate it from the rule which applies to gifts for pious uses. Gifts, therefore, conveyed to the Roman Catholic Church have usually been upheld as gifts for particular religious purposes, and they are included as charitable donations; and when such gifts are given to institutions which the law regards as intimately connected with the Church, such as schools, hospitals and asylums, they are regarded as gifts to institutions of public charity, inasmuch as they are open to the entire public indiscriminately, without regard to religious creed.[55] The fact that very few persons, other than members of the Church, avail themselves of the uses of its institutions does not affect its status as a public charity.[56]

It should be noted, however, that a restriction has been placed upon the extent to which the Roman Catholic Church is regarded as a public charity. The Supreme Court of Ohio has held that the Roman Catholic Church itself is not an institution of purely public charity under the statute allowing tax exemption, for while it teaches and practices charity as an essential part of its general program of church work, that is not its whole mission in the world. The Court stated that its chief and primary purpose and object was

[54] *Ibid.*, p. 826.

[55] Gerke *v.* Purcell (1874), 25 *Ohio State* 229; Humphries *v.* Little Sisters of the Poor (1876), 29 *Ohio State* 201; Mannix *v.* Purcell (1888), 46 Ohio State 102.

[56] The Ursuline Convent and Academy, for example, in the heart of Cleveland, is a school which is open to the public. Anyone may attend the same, Protestant or Catholic, and in this sense it is public, but it is not public in the sense that it belongs to the public. Cf. 7 *Ohio Jur.*, p. 147.

the teaching and extending of its recognized form of religious belief and worship, that it was a religious institution primarily, and that its charity was subordinate to its spiritual teachings.[57] It ruled, therefore, that parish houses, otherwise known as the residences of the priests and bishops of the Roman Catholic Church, are not exempt from taxation and legal assessments . . . although such places of residence are used by the priests and bishops for the discharge of many duties of a religious and charitable nature, which are imposed by the vows of their ordination and by the rules of the Church.[58]

Not only this kind of taxation in Ohio but also the inheritance tax has notably affected the Church's full right to property given to it for religious purposes. This is particularly true in cases of bequests made to the Church for the purpose of having Masses offered for the testator and for other designated persons. To qualify for exemption from inheritance tax, under the provisions of Section 5332 of the General Code, a church as an institution must not only be judged as an "institution for purposes of public charity only," but it is also required that the fund bequeathed to the Church be used for what the Courts actually judge to be purposes of public charity only. It is not sufficient that the use of the bequest be limited and restricted to the public charity activities of the church.[59] For example, a bequest to a church building fund is not exempt, for a church edifice is not considered to be used exclusively for purposes of public charity.[60] Bequests for Masses have been held to create a beneficial estate in the priest who will say the Masses, so as to be subject to the collateral inheritance tax.[61]

[57] Watterson *v.* Halliday (1907), 77 *Ohio State* 150.

[58] Cf. Syllabus to Watterson *v.* Halliday (1907), 77 *Ohio State* 150.

[59] Salisbury *v.* Department of Taxation (1951), 155 *Ohio State*, 615: Case was dismissed for want of debatable question.

[60] Cf. 38 *Ohio Jur.*, p 1264.

[61] Estate of Reilly: Roche, Executor and Trustee *v.* Department of Taxation of State of Ohio (1941), 138 *Ohio State* 145: It was

These restrictions, which have been imposed upon church property by the tax laws of Ohio, cannot be reconciled with the immunities and rights of the Church as stated in the sacred canons; but, although such restrictions interfere with the rights of the Church and of the donor to execute gifts according to the latter's desires, it seems that charitable trusts in favor of the Church have otherwise been carefully construed and executed according to equitable principles of common law. Courts have consistently shown a disposition to be liberal in the construction of such gifts, and have held them valid if they were possible of execution. They have declared only those gifts invalid and unenforceable which are impossible of execution. Furthermore, charity is one of those objects to which courts of equity have, since earliest times, applied principles of equity to make good those gifts which at law might be technically illegal and informal. Ohio legislation has thus provided for the adequate protection of the property of every social community and institution which subserves the public.[26]

held that where a testatrix by will set up trusts, the income or principal of which was to be paid in weekly installments to the pastors of designated churches for the purpose of saying Masses for herself, her family and relatives, such trusts are taxable successions under the provisions of Sec. 5332, General Code. (In this case the value of the trusts was set at $15,988. The inheritance tax upon this sum was set at $1,119.16).

Estate of Shanahan: Department of Taxation of Ohio *v.* Forsythe, Executrix (1953), 159 *Ohio State* 347: It was held that where a testator in his will directed his executrix to expend a portion of the testator's estate for Masses for himself and other members of his family according to the ritual of the Roman Catholic Church, such succession is taxable under the provisions of the statute, even though no particular priest was designated as the priest to say the Masses.

[62] McIntire *v.* City of Zanesville (1834), 9 Ohio Reports 203; Williams *v.* First Presbyterian Church (1853), 1 *Ohio State* 478.

CHAPTER VI

THE ADMINISTRATION OF CHURCH PROPERTY IN CANON LAW

ARTICLE I. THE APPOINTMENT OF ADMINISTRATORS

Property which is acquired and held by physical or moral persons may also be administered by them, for the status of ownership includes the right to the use and to all of the other fruitful advantages of property. These advantages can be fully obtained only through proper acts of administration. In the case of ecclesiastical goods such administration is necessary for the Church to accomplish successfully its divinely given end or purpose. The administration of church property comprises all of those acts which are required for the proper preservation and improvement of goods already acquired, and all acts which are necessary for collecting, conserving and applying the revenues and income accruing from these temporal goods.[1]

The right to administer property, as well as to acquire and to hold it, belongs to the Church as a native right independent of the civil authority.[2] Indeed, if individual physical persons are free to administer their goods independently, it follows *a fortiori* that such a right belongs to the Church.[3] Since, however, the ownership of church property is vested in the individual ecclesiastical person, such property must be administered by physical persons. All moral or legal persons in the Church are regarded as being equivalent to minors.[4] Ecclesiastical goods, therefore, are

[1] Cocchi, VI, p. 388, n. 198.

[2] Can. 1498, § 1.

[3] Wernz-Vidal, *Ius Canonicum ad Codicis Normam Exactum* (7 vols. in 8, Vol. IV, *De Rebus*, pars II, Romae: Apud Aedes Universitatis Gregorianae, 1934) IV, pars II, n. 747 (hereafter cited as Wernz-Vidal).

[4] Can. 100, § 3—Personae morales sive collegiales sive non collegiales minoribus aequiparantur.

regarded as the property of minors and, in the Church just as in other societies, the goods of minors are cared for by those who are legally appointed to administer them in keeping with the purposes for which they were acquired.[5]

Hence, ownership of church property is similar in effect to trusteeship. The legal person who holds the title to the goods is not free to use and to dispose of them in the same manner as the owner of private property, since ecclesiastical goods are acquired for specific purposes. By their very nature they are meant to serve the purposes of charity and religion, and those who are authorized to be their administrators act in the manner of trustees who exercise authority over church property by devoting it to the purposes for which the Church acquired it. In this sense they hold it in trust.[6] The Supreme Court of Ohio in the case, *Mannix v. Purcell,* alluded to this trust relationship when it accepted the canons and decrees of the Church as evidence that a trust existed. The Court stated that "the parties have gone back fifteen centuries into the laws and canons of the Church for proof of the nature of the tenure by which the Archbishop held the legal title to ecclesiastical property; and the proof is overwhelming that he was not invested with an absolute title to it as his own. It is practically conceded that he held it in trust...."[7]

The Sovereign Pontiff himself is not the owner of church property, but as Head of the Church he is declared in law to be the supreme administrator and dispenser of all ecclesiastical goods.[8] This right is derived from the plenitude of his power which embraces the final end of the Church as well as its means. The Pope in virtue of this power may

[5] Cocchi, *loc. cit.*

[6] Cf. Woywod, *A Practical Commentary on the Code of Canon Law* (revised by Callistus Smith, revised and enlarged edition, 2 vols., New York: Jos. F. Wagner, Inc., 1948), II, n. 1511 (hereafter cited as Woywod).

[7] Mannix *v.* Purcell at 136.

[8] Can. 1518—Romanus Pontifex est omnium bonorum ecclesiasticorum supremus administrator et dispensator.

dispense or dispose of all church property, even that which is owned by individual corporations if an urgent reason exists and the welfare or tranquillity of the Church Universal requires it.[9] In doing so, however, he is bound to provide for adequate compensation in the same manner as the secular authority is bound.[10] He may also condone usurpation, by the secular authority, of the property of subordinate ecclesiastical bodies. The Pope thus enjoys a right analogus to the right of eminent domain, which is based upon the legal maxim, "*Bonum privatum cedere debet bono publico.*"[11]

In practice the Roman Pontiff directly administers only the property of the Holy See, and he does this through offices and officials of the Roman Curia.[12] He has, however, communicated by law some of his powers to inferior or subordinate ordinaries. The Code states that it is the duty of the local ordinaries to watch carefully over the administration of all ecclesiastical property in their territories, except that which has been withdrawn from their jurisdiction, and that if lawful prescription gives the bishop more extensive rights to administer property otherwise not subject to his power, he may make use of this right.[13] Property which has been withdrawn from the bishop's jurisdiction is regarded as exempt. If, however, exempt religious or other exempt communities or individuals permit prescription against themselves, the original right revives, for as the pastor of the whole territory the bishop has the *intentio fundata in iure*.[14] By common law, therefore, he

[9] Augustine, *A Commentary on the New Code of Canon Law* (8 vols., Vol. VI, 2. ed., St. Louis: B. Herder Book Co., 1923) VI, 577 (hereafter cited as Augustine).

[10] Abbo-Hannan, II, 710.

[11] Augustine, VI, 578.

[12] Abbo-Hannan, II, 724, footnote n. 1.

[13] Can. 1519, § 1—Loci Ordinarii est sedulo advigilare administrationi omnium bonorum ecclesiasticorum quae in suo territorio sint nec ex eius iurisdictione fuerint subducta, salvis legitimis praescriptionibus, quae eidem potiora iura tribuant.

[14] Cocchi, VI, n. 200; Augustine, VI, 578-579; Cf. canons 531-537,

has the right of visitation of demanding reports, and of prescribing the method of administration.[15] In the exercise of this vigilance the local ordinaries are required to regulate the entire matter of the administration of ecclesiastical goods, and to give special opportune instructions in these matters, but such instructions must always be within the limits of the common law, and due regard must be given to the rights acquired by others, to legitimate customs and circumstances.[16]

Although canon 1519 imposes upon the ordinary the primary responsibility of superintending the administration of the property of the entire diocese, the law does not leave to him the fulfillment of this duty without the benefit of aid and counsel. In order, therefore, that the administration may be properly discharged, every ordinary is directed to establish in his episcopal city a board of administrators consisting of the president, who is the bishop himself, and two or more qualified men who are, if possible, experts also in civil law. The bishop is to select these men after hearing the chapter (the diocesan consultors); but if there be in the diocese a particular law or custom which provides an equally effective mode of administration, this may be retained.[17] In the selection of the members of this board the local ordinary must exclude those who are related to him in the first or second degree of consanguinity or affinity, unless he has obtained an indult from the Holy See

for the law governing the administration of goods of religious communities.

15 Vromant, *De Bonis Ecclesiae Temporalibus*, pp. 160-161, n. 181.

16 Can. 1519, § 2—Habita ratione iurium, legitimarum consuetudinum et circumstantiarum, Ordinarii, opportune editis peculiaribus instructionibus intra fines iuris communis, universum administrationis bonorum ecclesiasticorum negotium ordinandum curent.

17 Can. 1520, § 1—Ad hoc munus rite obeundum quilibet Ordinarius in sua civitate episcopali Consilium instituat, quod constet praeside, qui est ipsemet Ordinarius, et duobus vel pluribus viris idoneis, iuris etiam civilis, quantum fieri potest, peritis, ab ipso Ordinario, sudito Capitulo, eligendis, nisi iure vel consuetudine peculiari iam alio aequivalenti modo legitime fuerit provisum.

permitting it.[18] He may, however, choose laymen to serve as well as clerics, provided the laymen are Catholics.[19]

In the more important administrative business the local ordinaries are bound to consult the board of administrators. The members of this board act only in an advisory capacity, i.e., their vote is only consultative, unless their consent is required by the common law in particularly stated cases, or unless the charter of a foundation requires such consent.[20] Before assuming the duties of their office, however, the members must take an oath before the ordinary that they will efficiently and faithfully fulfill their office.[21]

Since it is the spirit of the law that each institution should have adequate administration, the Code also provides for such administration for all other churches or pious institutions which do not have administrators either by law or by the charters of their foundation. The ordinary is directed to choose prudent and capable men of good repute to administer the property of such institutions. These administrators are to serve for a term of three years, unless local circumstances counsel otherwise.[22] Examples of churches or pious institutions which are included under

[18] Can. 1520, § 2—Citra apostolicum indultum, ii a munere administratoris excluduntur, qui cum Ordinario loci primo vel secundo consanguinitatis vel affinitatis gradu coniuncti sint.

[19] Blat, *Commentarium Textus Codicis Iuris Canonici* (5 vols., Vol. III, Pars altera, Romae, 1923), III, Pars altera, n. 434; Augustine VI, 581.

[20] Can. 1520, § 3—Loci Ordinarius in administrativis actibus maioris momenti Consilium administrationis audire ne praetermittat; huius tamen sodales votum habent tantum consultivum, nisi iure communi in casibus specialiter expressis vel ex tabulis fundationis eorum consensus exigatur.

[21] Can. 1520, § 4—Sodales huius Consilii iusiurandum de munere bene ac fideliter adimplendo coram Ordinario emittant.

[22] Can. 1521, § 1—Praeter hoc dioecesanum Consilium administrationis, Ordinarius loci in administrationem bonorum quae ad aliquam ecclesiam vel locum pium pertinent et ex iure vel tabulis fundationis suum non habent administratorem, assumat viros providos, idoneos et boni testimonii, quibus, elapso triennio, alios sufficiat, nisi locorum circumstantiae aliud suadeant.

this canon are seminaries, hospitals, orphan asylums and associations of the faithful which have been canonically erected[23]

It is further required that if the charter of foundation or the will of the local ordinary should designate laymen to share in the administration of ecclesiastical property, the entire administration must be conducted in the name of the Church, and the right of the local ordinary to visit, to demand a regular account and to prescribe the method of administration must be safeguarded.[24] Canon 1183 treats of the *consilium fabricae* or the administrative council, which in the United States is usually called the board of trustees. If it is permitted to function, it must form a council under the presidency of the ecclesiastical administrator; its members are to be nominated by the ordinary or his delegate, and they can be removed by the same person for a grave reason. It is the duty of this board to administer the property of the Church in accordance with canons 1522 and 1523, but its members are never permitted to interfere in any of those matters which pertain to the spiritual office.[25]

Article II. Duties of Administrators

Section 1. General Administrative Duties

Acts of administration which are regularly required for

[23] Cf. Vromant, *op. cit.*, pp. 172-173, n. 197.

[24] Can. 1521, § 2—Quod si laicis partes quaedam in administratione bonorum ecclesiasticorum vel ex legitimo fundationis seu erectionis titulo vel ex Ordinarii loci voluntate competant, nihilominus universa administratio nomine Ecclesiae fiat, ac salvo iure Ordinarii visitandi, exigendi rationes et praescribendi modum administrationis.

[25] For an enumeration of particular spiritual matters which are exempt from such interference, cf. can. 1184.

Since the pastor is the administrator of the parish entrusted to him, canon 1521, § 1, does not require the local ordinary to appoint church committeemen to assist the pastor in the administration. The local ordinary is free to provide for their appointment in accordance with the discretion granted to him by the III Plenary Council of Baltimore. Cf. *Acta et Decreta,* n. 287, I.

the ordinary care of church property may be performed by the administrators without the permission of any higher authority. Among such acts are included the acceptance of ordinary donations; the collections of debts, rents, interest, or dividends; the making of those contracts and payments for the ordinary maintenance of the church and its personnel; the opening of checking accounts to facilitate these payments.[26] Since the performance of these acts is left to their own discretion, all administrators of ecclesiastical property, whether they are appointed by law, or charter, or a mandate of the local ordinary, are required to fulfill their responsibility with true diligence and in a conscientious manner. Before they assume their office, therefore, the administrators designated in canon 1521 are obliged to perform the following duties:

(1) They must take an oath, in the presence of the local ordinary or the rural dean, that they will efficiently and faithfully attend to their work of administration;

(2) they must prepare an accurate itemized inventory of immovable property and of precious and other movable property with a description of it and an estimate of its value; or a previously made inventory must be accepted with an account of the property which has been acquired or lost since it was made. This inventory must be signed by the administrators, and

(3) one copy of this inventory must be filed in the archives of the council of administration, and another in the archives of the diocesan curia. In both copies there must be noted whatever change may have occurred in the status of the property.[27]

[26] Cf. Vromant, *op. cit.*, p. 161, n. 182.

[27] Can. 1522—Antequam administratores bonorum ecclesiasticorum, de quibus in can. 1521, suum munus ineant:

1°. Debent se bene et fideliter administraturos coram Ordinario loci vel vicario foraneo iureiurando cavere;

2°. Fiat accuratum ac distinctum inventarium, ab omnibus subscri-

The degree of responsibility which administrators of church property are under obligation to exercise is compared with the diligence of a good householder. In particular they must:

(1) Guard against the property being lost or damaged;

(2) observe the requirements of both canon law and civil law, as well as the requirements specified by the founder or the donor, or imposed by legitimate authority;

(3) collect the revenues and income diligently and promptly, keeping them safely and using them in accordance with the intention of the founder or with established laws or norms;

(4) invest the surplus revenue of a church for the benefit of the church itself, after obtaining the consent of the ordinary;

(5) keep an accurate record of receipts and expenditures;

(6) arrange in proper order the documents and papers on which the property rights of the church are based and file them in the archives or in a suitable and adequate safe; and, when it can readily be done, deposit authentic copies of them in the archives or safe of the diocesan curia.[28]

bendum, rerum immobilium, rerum mobilium pretiosarum aliarumve cum descriptione atque aestimatione earundem; vel factum antea inventarium acceptetur, adnotatis rebus quae interim amissae vel acquisitae fuerint;

3°. Huius inventarii alterum exemplar conservetur in tabulario administrationis, alterum in archivo Curiae; et in utroque quaelibet immutatio adnotetur quam patrimonium subire contingat.

[28] Can. 1523, 1°-6°—Administratores bonorum ecclesiasticorum diligentia boni patrisfamilias suum munus implere tenentur; ac proinde debent:

1°. Vigilare ne bona ecclesiastica suae curae concredita quoque modo pereant aut detrimentum capiant;

2°. Praescripta servare iuris tam canonici quam civilis, aut quae a fundatore vel donatore vel legitima auctoritate imposita sint;

3°. Reditus bonorum ac proventus accurate et iusto tempore exigere exactosque loco tuto servare et secundum fundatoris mentem aut

The requirements of canon 1523 are binding on pastors in virtue of canon 1182, § 1, and on church committeemen in virtue of canon 1184. Furthermore, the III Plenary Council of Baltimore specifically required adequate fire insurance, thus giving special force to the obligation of safeguarding property as imposed in canon 1523, 1°.[29] The Council also required that the deeds to parish property should be drawn up under the supervision of experts and that they be placed in the archives of the diocese; other documents affecting the property or interests of the parish were to be kept in an iron safe belonging to the parish.[30] These requirements have not lost their force, except that which provides for the filing of the original deeds in the archives of the diocese; canon 1523, 6°, supposes that copies will be filed there. There also remain in force the requirements of the III Plenary Council which provide for an annual revision of the inventory of all parochial property inclusive of the cemetery. The pastor or administrator and the church committeemen must sign this document and send it to the chancellor.[31] A copy of such an inventory, annually revised and signed, must also be kept in the files of the respective churches or pious places, and it must be presented to an incoming pastor or administrator by his predecessor or by the rural dean.[32]

Bishops are required to draw up an authentic inventory of all sacred furnishings, stating accurately the date on

statutas leges vel normas impendere;

4°. Pecuniam ecclesiae, quae de expensis supersit et utiliter collocari potest, de consensu Ordinarii, in emolumentum ipsius ecclesiae occupare;

5°. Accepti et expensi libros bene ordinatos habere;

6°. Documenta et instrumenta, quibus iura ecclesiae in bona nituntur, rite ordinare et in ecclesiae archivo vel armario convenienti et apto custodire; authentica vero eorum exemplaria, ubi commode fieri potest, in archivo vel armario Curiae deponere.

29 *Acta et Decreta*, n. 283.

30 *Acta et Decreta*, nos. 270, 278, 282.

31 *Acta et Decreta*, n. 276.

32 *Loc. cit.*

which they were acquired and clearly determining which of them have been acquired, not from the Church's income and revenues, but from his own estate or through donations made to him personally; otherwise all are presumed bought with the income of the church.[33]

To provide for the security of church property, even before the civil law, cardinals, residential bishops and other clerics who are incumbents of a benefice are duty bound to execute a last will or other documents in a form recognized as valid by the civil law. As soon as they take possession of their benefice they are required to execute an appointment, valid in civil law, of a person of good reputation as specified in canon 380, whose duty it is, in the event of death, to take possession of the sacred furnishings, books, documents and other things belonging to the church, and to deliver them to their rightful claimants.[34]

All administrators who have the duty of employing workingmen are obligated to pay them just and decent wages. This rule applies especially to clerics, religious and administrators of ecclesiastical goods, who must provide that the workingmen are free to perform their religious duties, and must prevent them from being burdened with work which is beyond their strength or which is not suited to their age or sex.[35]

Section 2. Special Duties of Administrators

Both ecclesiastical and lay administrators are required to submit an annual report to the local ordinary of their administration, with every custom to the contrary ruled

[33] Can. 1299, § 3.

[34] Can. 1301.

[35] Can. 1524—Omnes et praesertim clerici, religiosi ac rerum ecclesiasticarum administratores, in operum locatione debent assignare operariis honestam iustamque mercedem; curare ut iidem pietati, idoneo temporis spatio, vacent; nullo pacto eos abducere a domestica cura parsimoniaeque studio, neque plus eisdem imponere operis quam vires ferre queant neque id genus quod cum aetate sexuque dissideat.

out and reprobated. This report must be presented by all, whether they are administrators of a church, including the cathedral church, or of a canonically established pious place or of a confraternity. If under particular law a report must also be submitted to others specifically designated, the ordinary or his delegate must be included among these, and any specification made for the purpose of excluding the local ordinary is void.[36] Included among those who must make this report to the ordinary are the administrators of certain religious communities. Canon 535, § 1, requires the superioress of every monastery of nuns, even exempt, to submit an account of her administration annually, or even more often if the constitutions prescribe it. This account must be given to the regular superior also if the monastery be subject to regulars. In the other institutes of women the account of the administration of the property constituted by the dowries of the women religious must be given to the local ordinary on the occasion of the visitation, or even more often if the ordinary considers it necessary.[37] This is the extent of the rights of the ordinary concerning the management of property which belongs entirely to congregations approved by the Holy See.[38] The local ordinary, however, has the right to inquire into the economic status of the houses of diocesan congregations located in his diocese. He also has the right to require an account of the goods and property administered by the religious of all orders and congregations if such goods and property were given for divine worship or charitable pur-

[36] Canon 1525: § 1. Reprobata contraria consuetudine, administratores tam ecclesiastici quam laici cuiusvis ecclesiae etiam cathedralis aut loci pii canonice erecti aut confraternitatis singulis annis officio tenentur reddendi rationem administrationis Ordinario loci.

§. Si ex peculiari iure aliis ad id designatis ratio reddenda sit, tunc etiam Ordinarius loci vel eius delegatus cum his admittatur, ea lege ut aliter factae liberationes ipsis administratoribus minime suffragentur.

[37] Can. 535, § 2.

[38] Creusen-Ellis-Garesché, *Religious Men and Women in the Code* (4. ed., Milwaukee: Bruce, 1940), n. 167.

poses to be applied in the diocese, as stated in canon 533.[39] With these exceptions, therefore, the religious orders of men and all congregations, both of men and women, under papal law manage their own financial affairs and the property belonging to the community according to their constitutions, without being obliged to make a report to the bishop of the diocese.

Administrators of church property are forbidden to institute a suit or to undertake a defense to a suit in the name of the Church unless they have obtained written permission from the local ordinary or at least, in the case of an emergency, from the rural dean, who shall immediately inform the ordinary of the permission given.[40] If they fail to obtain the necessary permission in this or in any act which exceeds the limits of ordinary administration they act invalidly.[41] In such cases they are bound in conscience to restitution for any loss sustained. If they relinquish an office which they have either explicitly or tacitly assumed, and thereby cause loss to the Church, they are likewise bound to restitution. This rule holds even though they were not bound to act as administrators by reason of an ecclesiastical benefice or office.[42]

The Church is not responsible for contracts made by administrators who lacked the permission of the competent superior except when and to the extent that it has profited from them.[43] Since the local ordinary is the superintendent

[39] Can. 535, § 3.

[40] Can. 1526—Administratores litem nomine ecclesiae ne inchoent vel contestentur, nisi licentiam obtinuerint scripto datam Ordinarii loci, aut saltem, si res urgeat, vicarii foranei, qui statim Ordinarium de concessa licentia certiorem reddere debet.

[41] Can. 1527, § 1—Nisi prius ab Ordinario loci facultatem impetraverint, scriptis dandam, administratores invalide actus ponunt qui ordinariae administrationis fines et modum excedant.

[42] Can. 1528—Etsi administrationem non teneantur titulo beneficii vel officii ecclesiastici, administratores qui munus expresse vel tacite susceptum arbitratu suo dimittunt ita ut damnum exinde ecclesiae obveniat, ad restitutionem tenentur.

[43] Can. 1527, § 2—Ecclesia non tenetur respondere de contractibus

of the administration of all church property in his diocese, and thus has the primary responsibility, the Church is careful to insist upon his formal and written consent for all acts of administration which are classified as extraordinary. These acts include all alienation of church property; the acceptance or the refusal of a gift or a bequest; the purchase of land; the construction of new buildings or extensive repairs on old buildings; the opening of a cemetery; the investment of any kind of capital, whether liquid or stable; the establishment of a school or any other similar parochial institution; and the taking up of special collections.[44]

In addition to the permission of the local ordinary as required for acts of extraordinary administration it is often necessary, in many of these acts, to enter into contracts for the protection of all parties concerned. In this regard, therefore, the Church simplifies matters by canonically adopting the civil law of the different countries for contracts concerning ecclesiastical property and the rights connected with it. Whatever the civil law of the territory provides generally and specifically regarding contracts shall be observed as if enacted by canon law in ecclesiastical matters with the same effects, unless it is contrary to the divine law or unless other provisions are made by canon law.[45] The civil law prescribes formalities or rules which must be observed in order that a contract be valid. These formalities may concern all contracts in general or only a certain class of contracts. Those contracts which have obtained special names in law, such as contracts of sale, rent, lease,

ab administratoribus sine licentia competentis Superioris initis, nisi quando et quatenus in rem suam versum sit.

[44] Cf. Vromant, *De Bonis Ecclesiae Temporalibus*, p. 194, n. 223; cf. also Abbo-Hannan, II, p. 731.

[45] Can. 1529—Quae ius civile in territorio statuit de contractibus tam in genere, quam in specie, sive nominatis sive innominatis, et de solutionibus, eadem iure canonico in materia ecclesiastica iisdem cum effectibus serventur, nisi iuri divino contraria sint aut aliud iure canonico caveatur.

etc., are referred to in canon 1529 as *nominati.* Nameless contracts, or *innominati,* belong to the fourfold class of: *do ut des, facio ut facias, do ut facias, facio ut des.* Regardless of the kind of contracts involved, the formalities which concern their validity and lawfulness must be observed even if the subject matter, or the consideration, or the contracting parties belong to the Church.[46] It is obvious that one exception must be made, namely, when such formalities violate the divine law. The other exception is exemplified in canon 536, wherein the Church has ruled otherwise concerning the formalities of contracts affecting members of religious communities. Without the permission of the legitimate superior any contract which is made to alienate church property, movable or immovable, is invalid.

Besides this permission for acts of alienation there is also required a written appraisal of the property by reliable experts as well as a justifying reason, i.e., an urgent need, the evident advantage of the Church, or piety. The Church furthermore insists that other opportune precautions needed to prevent injury to the Church shall not be overlooked, but shall be specified by the respective superiors.[47]

The phrase, "acts of alienation," as employed by the Code, includes not only sale, but any other contract by

[46] Cf. Augustine, VI, 590-591.

[47] Can. 1530, § 1—Salvo praescripto can. 1281, § 1, ad alienandas res ecclesiasticas immobiles aut mobiles, quae servando servari possunt, requiritur:

1°. Aestimatio rei a probis peritis scripto facta;

2°. Iusta causa, idest urgens necessitas, vel evidens utilitas Ecclesiae, vel pietas;

3°. Licentia legitimi Superioris, sine qua alienatio invalida est;

§ 2. Aliae quoque opportunae cautelae, ab ipsomet Superiore pro diversis adiunctis praescribendae, ne omittantur, ut Ecclesiae damnum vitetur.

Canon 1281, § 1, rules that important relics and images of great value and other relics or images which are honored in some church by way of great veneration of the people, cannot validly be disposed of, nor transferred perpetually to another church, without the permission of the Apostolic See.

which a third party acquires any right to the real or personal property belonging to an ecclesiastical legal person. Inasmuch as the ownership or usufruct or some right is transferred to another by the act of alienation, there results a certain weakening of the assets of the moral person, thereby making them less secure and placing a burden upon the Church.[48] This is why the Church protects its property with detailed laws controlling alienation. In addition to the conditions mentioned above, the Code states that property shall not be alienated for a price less than that specified in the estimate.[49] This estimate must be made by at least two appraisers, and each may submit his written appraisal separately.[50] Furthermore, the alienation should be executed by way of a public auction, or at least it should be announced publicly unless circumstances suggest otherwise, and the goods to be disposed of should be awarded to whoever, all things considered, makes the higher bid.[51] This sum of money obtained from the alienation must be invested safely and profitably.[52]

The lawful superior whose permission is required for the validity of acts of alienation depends upon the value of the property involved. Canon 1532, § 1, of the present Code states that if the property is a precious object, or if its value exceeds 30,000 lire or francs, the permission of the Holy See is necessary. It must be noted, however, that the Sacred Consistorial Congregation, on October 18, 1952,

[48] Cf. Woywod, II, 208; Cf. Augustine, VI, 593.

[49] Can. 1531, § 1—Res alienari minore pretio non debet quam quod in aestimatione indicatur.

[50] Cf. Blat, *Commentarium Textus Codicis Iuris Canonici,* III Pars altera, n. 446.

[51] Can. 1531, § 2—Alienatio fiat per publicam licitationem aut saltem nota reddatur, nisi aliud circumstantiae suadeant; et res ei concedatur qui, omnibus perpensis, plus obtulerit.

If the local ordinary judges that a secret sale would more favorably serve the interests of the Church, the public auction could be lawfully omitted. Cf. Vermeersch-Creusen, II, n. 853.

[52] Can. 1531, § 3—Pecunia ex alienatione percepta caute, tuto et utiliter in commodum Ecclesiae collocetur.

issued a Notification by which it reduced the rates concerning alienations and debts until new dispositions are made. This Notification contains a list of countries and the sums of money, in actual currency, which are to be considered for the respective countries as the limits beyond which the permission of the Holy See is required according to canons 534, § 1, and 1532, § 1, n. 2. The amount which was determined for North and Central America was 5,000 U.S. Dollars. It was stated that this disposition applied to all ecclesiastical bodies existing in the territory, whatever might be the Congregation of the Roman Curia on which they depended.[53]

Canon 1532, § 2, states that, if the value of the property does not exceed 1,000 lire or francs, it is the local ordinary who gives the permission after he has heard the council of administration, unless the property is of very slight value and the interested parties give their consent. Canon 1532, § 3, states that, if the value of the property is between 1,000 and 30,000 lire or francs, it is again the local ordinary who gives permission, provided that he has obtained the consent of the cathedral chapter (diocesan consultors), of the council of administration and of the interested parties. According to the Notification cited above, however, the sum of "a thousand lire or francs" mentioned in canon 1532, § 2, is to be taken as a sum equal to one-thirtieth of the value indicated in the table for the various countries. For the United States, therefore, that amount is approximately $167.00.[54]

According to canon 1532, § 4, all of the formalities required in canons 1530-1532 must be observed not only in connection with the alienating of church property in the restricted sense but also in connection with the making of any contract which might endanger the condition of the Church. A contract, therefore, which would place the

[53] Bouscaren, *The Canon Law Digest* (3 vols. and Supplement through 1953, Milwaukee, Wis: The Bruce Publishing Co., 1934-1943-1954), Supplement under can. 1532 (hereafter cited as *Digest*).

[54] *Loc. cit.*

Church in a long-term debt is included under the norm of this canon. When permission is sought for the making of loans the current existing indebtedness of the respective ecclesiastical body must be specified.[55] Canon 1538 states that if there be a legitimate reason for church property to be pledged or mortgaged, or if debts must be contracted, the competent superior must demand that a previous hearing be given to all interested parties, and he must see to it that the debts are paid as soon as possible. In doing this the ordinary must determine the annual rate at which the debts are to be liquidated.

The Church permits the sale and leasing of its property, but not without restrictions. Immovable goods may not be sold or leased to the administrators of the same church or to persons related to them in the first or second degree of consanguinity or affinity.[56] If land is leased to others it must be done according to the provisions of canon 1531, § 2, i.e., it shall not be leased except by way of public auction or other public announcement, unless special circumstances make a different method advisable. In addition to this, provisions must always be made for the protection of boundaries, for an adequate maintenance, and for the payment of rent, with appropriate guaranties for the observance of these provisions.[57] Canon 1541, § 2, lays down further rules concerning acts of leasing. It first states that canon 1497 must be observed. This canon forbids the holder of a benefice to receive payment of the rent for over six months in advance when property of the benefice is leased. Canon 1541, § 2, states that:

(1) If the value of the lease is in excess of 30,000 lire or francs (now, however, $5,000 for the United States) and the term of the lease is more than nine years, there is required the *beneplacitum apostolicum.* If the term is not more than nine years, the local ordinary's permission is

[55] Abbo-Hannan, II, 739.
[56] Can. 1540.
[57] Can. 1541, § 1.

required together with the consent of the diocesan consultors, the consent of the diocesan council of administration, and the consent of any interested parties.

(2) If the value is between 1,000 and 30,000 lire or francs (now, however, between $167 and $5,000 for the United States) and the term exceeds nine years, the permission of the local ordinary and the consent of those stated above (except that of the Holy See) are required; if the term does not exceed nine years the permission of the local ordinary is required after consultation with the diocesan council of administration, and also the consent of any interested parties unless the term is a very small one.

(3) If the value does not exceed 1,000 lire or francs (now, however, about $167.00 for the United States) but the term is longer than nine years, there is required the permission of the local ordinary after consultation with the diocesan council of administration, and also the consent of any interested parties. Finally, if the term does not exceed nine years the lease can be made by the competent administrators after notifying the ordinary.

The canonical rules which have been stated in this chapter regarding the administration of church property are those rules in the Code which can be affected by the legislation of civil authority. To protect its rights in property matters and to keep those rights secure the Church is always concerned about the enactments of the civil laws which touch its essential hierarchial discipline. The purpose, therefore, of the following, final chapter of this work will be to examine the property legislation of the State of Ohio insofar as it affects the administration of church property, and to discover thereby to what extent the laws of the Code can operate within the framework of Ohio legislation in safeguarding the rights and powers which are deemed necessary and desirable for church authorities.

CHAPTER VII

THE LAW OF OHIO GOVERNING THE ADMINISTRATION OF CHURCH PROPERTY

The law of Ohio, as well as the Code of Canon Law, contains provisions for the administration of property which has been conveyed to religious societies, churches, or associations whether incorporated or not. The administrators of this property are called trustees and the civil law states that "property conveyed in trust for the use of such societies shall be held by the trustee or trustees so appointed and their successors appointed as provided in the instrument creating the trust, or in case no provision is made in such instrument, then by such successor or successors as are appointed by a competent court. . . ."[1] Since it is generally held that a trust for the benefit of the public attaches to property secured by corporations and unincorporated societies organized for charitable and religious purposes, this property so secured and used is not subject to levy and sale in execution where such sale would defeat the trust and destroy the public purpose for which the property was donated or secured.[2] The courts, therefore, claim supervision over the property rights of religious societies to the extent that they will prevent the abuse, perversion or destruction of a trust for public worship and other charitable purposes. They will thereby protect the rights of members of a religious society to use and enjoy its property according to the terms of the trust under which it is held, and according to the rules of the society and the regulations enacted by the trustees or other governing body. Section 10021 of the Ohio General Code provides that "the trustee or trustees, for the time being, of any such religious society may defend and prosecute suits and do all other

[1] *Page's Ohio General Code,* § 10,022.

[2] 17 *Ohio Jur.*, p. 894, § 294; Minor v. Smith (1861), 13 Ohio State, 79.

acts for the protection, improvement and preservation of the property that individuals can do in relation to their individual property." The law imposes certain duties upon these trustees and also invests them with necessary powers to insure the proper execution of their acts of administration. These duties and powers must be examined if one is to discover to what extent they are similar to those which the Code of Canon Law provides for the administrators of church property.

ARTICLE I. DUTIES IMPOSED UPON TRUSTEES BY THE LAW OF OHIO

Since the trustee holds property entirely for the benefit of others, the law binds him with the duty of administering the trust most scrupulously in the interest of the beneficiary. This duty is referred to as the trustee's duty of loyalty. Thus the law provides that the trustee has no interest in the property which his own creditors can reach by execution, by proceedings in bankruptcy, or by any other means. Execution cannot be levied upon such property, and it is in no way subject to the trustee's own debts.[3] Loyalty also forbids trustees to profit personally through the administration of the trust, for "all of their power, influence and skill is to be used in favor of the beneficial

[3] Cf. 40 *Ohio Jur.*, § 131; In the case, *Mannix v. Purcell*, there was evidence tending to show that the Archbishop and his Vicar General represented to depositors that the entire church property was bound for repayment of deposits as well as payment of interest, but the Court stated: "The law will not permit a trustee thus to talk away the trust estate. It is required of the trustee in this case, as in all others, that he be faithful." The trust property, therefore, did not pass to the assignee for the benefit of the trustee's creditors. Cf. 46 Ohio State 102.

In the case, *Cincinnati v. Cameron* (1864), 7 Am. L. Rep. 592, the Court said that "trust property generally is not subject to seizure at the instance of a creditor of a trustee." In the case, *Manley v. Hunt* (1824), 1 Ohio Reports 257, it was declared that "it would be productive of much mischief and injustice to make trust estates liable to judgments against the trustee. Such a principle never has been, and we trust never will be, recognized in this state."

owners, and not for personal gain."[4] The trustees are forbidden to acquire an interest in the property, or to purchase it at their own sale, directly or indirectly[5]

In the administration of the trust, therefore, the trustee is bound to exercise that degree of care and skill which an ordinarily prudent man would exercise in dealing with his own property. "It has never been the policy to treat persons holding fiduciary relations as gratuitious bailees or trustees, but as bailees for hire, and bound to the highest degree of good faith and diligence and to the exercise of that reasonable skill which is commensurate with the character of the trust they have undertaken and for which they receive a reasonable compensation."[6] There is a presumption in favor of the trustee to the effect that he has satisfied the necessary standard of care, until the contrary is shown. When trustees act within the scope of their authority and exercise such prudence, care and diligence as men ordinarily manifest in like matters of their own, they should not be held accountable for losses happening from their management of the trust funds. The maxim that every person is presumed to know the law is not always applicable to trustees; on the contrary, they may be exonerated from losses resulting from their ignorance of the law in cases where they exercised proper diligence and precaution, and acted upon the advice of counsel.[7] This, however, does not mean that merely good intentions are sufficient to free the trustee from responsibility for negligent or improvident conduct. Since he must always administer the property for the benefit of the *cestui que trust* he is bound to act prudently to protect the trust property from loss or damage. Thus he may not abandon the property or release the securities of a loan or enter any contract which would destroy the interest of the beneficiary. Such actions, though

[4] Berkemeyer *v.* Kellerman (1877), 32 Ohio State 239.
[5] *Page's Ohio General Code,* §§ 10,506-47 10,506-49.
[6] Dayton *v.* Bartlett (1882), 38 Ohio State 357.
[7] Syllabus to Miller *v.* Proctor (1870), 20 Ohio State 442.

performed without dishonest intentions, would not be considered reasonable and would not be enforced.[8]

When the trust has been assumed, the first duty of the trustee is to take possession of the property and to keep control of it. Every fiduciary under the jurisdiction of the probate court is required to file an inventory within three months after his appointment, setting forth all property, real and personal, with its value and the yearly rental of real estate.[9] This inventory is subject to attack within six months by interested persons. After he has taken possession, the trustee must not only retain it, but he must also secure it by collecting any rents or profits which might accrue and, in the case of intangibles, is obliged to collect or convert them into proper investments and to keep these securities in a safe manner, dealing with them with the utmost fairness.[10]

After he has filed the required inventory, the trustee is bound to keep a careful account of his administration of the trust. He has a duty to give reasonable information

[8] Watterson *v.* Ury (1891), 5 Ohio Circuit Court 347: A grant of real estate, purporting to be upon a valuable consideration to be held by the "grantee, his heirs and assigns forever as a burial ground for Roman Catholics," containing a covenant to "forever warrant and defend said premises with the appurtenances against the lawful claims of all persons whomsoever, to be held by such grantee in trust for the Roman Catholics of Columbus, Ohio," and containing no words of forfeiture or re-entry, is not a grant upon condition; and a discontinuance or diversion of the use contemplated by the grant will not entitle the heirs of the grantor to recover the granted premises. (Cf. Syllabus). Thus the Court would not permit Bishop Watterson, as trustee, to abandon the *trust res.*

Moeller *v.* Poland (1909), 80 Ohio State 418: Where, with respect to the disposition of the property of the trust, a trustee's judgment is finally to control, and yet there be devolved upon him by the nature of the trust the duty to take reasonable means to enable him to arrive at a correct and reasonable judgment, and such duty be entirely neglected by the trustee, the mere presence of good intention and absence of bad motive will not be sufficient to relieve him of a charge of breach of trust. (Cf. Syllabus).

[9] *Page's Ohio General Code,* §§ 10,506-84.

[10] 40 *Ohio Jur.,* § 139.

concerning the trust property, to permit an inspection of the accounts and to answer inquiries, within reasonable limits, concerning his management and control of the property. He can be required to give, at stated intervals, a report or account to the proper court or to the beneficiaries. This duty will definitely be enforced against an express trustee, and it has been required as well against a constructive trustee and a resulting trustee. The parties to the trust, however, may, by agreement, effectuate what amounts to a virtual private accounting.[11] It seems that this kind of accounting would be sufficient in the case of a bishop who acts as trustee of diocesan property in Ohio because of the wide discretion in management and control which he is allowed to exercise. In keeping, however, with his duty, there is nothing to prevent the courts from requiring a detailed and public account of his administration. It should be noted here that the inventory of property and the report required by the civil law can be given in good order by the local ordinary inasmuch as canon 1522, 1°, requires an inventory, and canon 1525 requires an annual report, both of which must be given to the local ordinary as superintending the administration of the property of the entire diocese.

The civil law forbids the trustee to delegate his discretionary power or personal duties, i.e., those acts which he should perform himself. Once he has accepted the trust it is generally held that he cannot delegate to another the administration of the property. He may, however, delegate any merely ministerial act. Thus, lawyers, brokers, and priests in parishes may act as agents of the bishop, and if the terms of the trust instrument permit a delegation of the trust powers there can be no objection to it.[12] By virtue, therefore, of the degree of control which is vested in the bishop, as trustee, this power of delegation is implied in the trust instrument.

Although it is the trustee's duty to control and possess

[11] *Ibid.*, §§ 133, 134. [12] Cf. *Ibid.*, § 131.

the property, this does not mean that he must retain a personal possession. He may lease realty and place personalty in the hands of agents or employees, and he may deposit money in a bank. Trust money or personal property in his possession should be kept separate and not be mixed with his own, and properties of separate trusts in the same trustee should not be mixed. Whenever the trustee purchases land for the trust, buys stock, bonds, or other securities, or opens bank deposits, he should always earmark the property by making it evident that the title has been taken in his capacity as trustee.[13]

After he has taken possession of the property the trustee must make the *trust res* produce an income. This is the basis of his duty to invest and to reinvest. His authority to make investments may be derived from the trust instrument itself, or it may be implied from the general power of management which he possesses. Such investments must be made within a reasonable time, and the guiding principles in making them are the safety of the principal and the securing of as large an income as possible, provided it is compatible with safety and protection. The failure by the trustee to make proper investments, or any violation of his duty in the manner of investment, will make him liable for any loss incurred.[14] This liability is not always excused by the fact that he sought the advice of counsel or employed a broker. He cannot shift the responsibility upon others, but he himself must determine the safety of the investment. His investigation, though it may not reveal the weakness of the investment being considered, may, in a large measure, induce the court to relieve the trustee from liability because of the strong evidence of prudence and good faith employed by him.[15] Thus the trustee will satisfy the requirements of the law in the matter of making investments and will escape liability if he

[13] *Ibid.*, pp. 376-377.

[14] *Page's Ohio General Code*, §§ 10,506-46.

[15] Willis *v.* Braucher (1909), 79 Ohio State 290.

exercises the same degree of diligence and care that a man of ordinary prudence would exercise in the management and investment of his own money. If he then should fail to make wise decisions and to exercise sound judgment, he will be protected.[16]

Since the first duty of the trustee, on his appointment, is to collect all of the property and to secure its possession, he is the proper person to bring any suit which may become necessary for this purpose, and he has a duty to bring such suits in the administration of the trust. Suits must be brought in the trustee's own name. The legislature, in making provision for an action to be brought in the name of the real party in interest, makes an exception with respect to a trustee in an express trust by providing that "he may bring an action without joining with him the person for whose benefit it is prosecuted."[17] In the proper management of the trust he may bring any action necessary to protect or defend such property or to recover possession of such property, or compensation for it, when it has been unlawfully appropriated by another.

A trustee "who has accepted a trust is bound not only to bring necessary suits, but also to defend the trust property against suits brought against it, and he may therefore charge upon it the proper expenses of such defense."[18] The

[16] In the case, *Miller v. Proctor* (1870), 20 Ohio State 442, the fiduciaries, in good faith, took a mortgage on property, but made a mistake of law concerning firm creditor's rights. The Court stated that "it is manifest, however, that they acted in utter ignorance of the law—or rather, the rule of equity—by which such property is subjected, as personal assets, to the payment of partnership debts to the exclusion of liens created thereon by the individual members of the firm. It is admitted that they acted in good faith and exercised their best judgment. They followed the advice of their counsel.... Would it be just, under such circumstances, to hold them accountable for their ignorance of this recondite... principle which, though established as law in Ohio, is said to be denied in some other states?"

[17] *Page's Ohio General Code*, §§ 11,241 & 11,244.

[18] Andrews' Executors *v.* Andrews' Administrators (1857), 7 *Ohio State* 143; The Court stated that "the idea that the law should imperiously thrust an onerous duty upon the trustee having, in general,

trustee's duty to defend is coextensive with his trust. If he has reasonably brought or defended a suit and lost the decision he may, and is under duty to, carry the case to the higher court, on either appeal or error. It is more than a privilege; it is a duty where the decision is destructive of the trust.[19]

ARTICLE II. POWERS GRANTED TO TRUSTEES

All administrators of property must not only be charged with definite duties, such as those emphasized in the foregoing article, but they must also be granted certain powers or the authority to perform certain specified acts necessary for the effective administration of the trust property. The trustee derives his powers from two sources. They are either conferred expressly by the instrument, in which case they are called *special* powers, or they are found to exist in the trustee by implication of law, and thus they are referred to as *general* powers. They are also called *discretionary* powers when they are annexed to the trust and may be exercised or not, entirely in the discretion of the named trustee, and powers *in trust,* which are imperative powers and which will therefore be exercised by a successor in trust, since they are not personal in character.[20]

The powers of the trustee are affected by the extent of the estate given to him. He must take the amount of estate necessary to enable him to perform the trust. Likewise, the trustee usually has the custody and possession of the *trust res,* thus making it possible to exercise his powers over the property without hindrance.[21] In respect to diocesan property held by the bishop, as trustee, and prop-

no personal interest in the existence of the trust, and make him personally responsible for the expenses necessarily accruing in the discharge of that duty, is wholly inadmissible."

[19] Gearhart *v.* Richardson (1924), Ohio State 418: Both the trial court and the court of appeals decided against the trustee; still the Court said that it was his duty to appeal.

[20] Cf. 40 *Ohio Jur.*, § 161.

[21] *Loc. cit.*

erty held in trust for incorporated religious communities, it must always be remembered that the trust instrument is only one factor which may determine and express the powers of the trustee. The law permits additional powers which broaden the scope of management and control, and which are determined by the rules of the religious society itself and the regulations enacted by the trustee, or trustees, or other governing body.[22]

Section 1. The Power of the Trustee to Incur Expenses

The trustee has the power to incur any expenses which he finds necessary and appropriate in the performance of his duties. At the beginning of his trust duties he may find it necessary to create obligations in collecting and reducing to his custody and possession the *corpus* of the trust estate. He has the power to do this, and he also has the power to make the necessary expenditures to preserve the *trust res,* to make it productive, and to perform those duties which are expressly required and which would entail incidental expenses, such as costs of sale, lease, etc. The trustee may incur all of the proper costs, fees, and expenses which are incidental to maintaining and defending suits, as well as all charges which are necessary to hire brokers and agents in the administration of the trust. He may not, however, incur expenses by hiring others to perform duties which he himself should perform.

The trust instrument usually contains an authorization to the trustee respecting necessary repairs and permanent improvements of the property. In the absence of such a grant of power, the same power will usually be implied from the trust instrument or from the trustee's duty to care for and preserve the *trust res.* If the trust is to continue over a considerable period of time, a permanent improvement would be more justifiable than if it had but a short time to continue. In the case, *Mannix v. Purcell,* it was held that the power to charge the property for ex-

[22] 35 *Ohio Jur.,* § 31.

penses for preservation, improvement or repairs in favor of the party performing the labor was incidental to the ownership of the title.[23]

Section 2. The Power of the Trustee to Sell, Lease, or Encumber

The trustee's powers and duties with respect to the property in his possession are generally to hold and care for it, to collect its rents, earnings, or profits. There is no power presumed to exist in him to sell the property. The presumption is very likely to the contrary, in keeping with his duty to keep the property secure. In the absence, therefore, of a provision in the trust instrument conferring this power of sale upon him, or of facts justifying the implication of the power, the exercise of it would constitute a breach of trust. In many cases the trust instrument does not contain any delegation to the trustee of a power to sell, but in order to carry out his obligation it is necessary that he have this power. In such cases the power may be implied; but the power to hold, manage and control, expressly conferred upon the trustee, is not sufficient, of itself, to authorize the trustee to make sales of the property. Such a power, however, taken in conjunction with the remainder of the trust instrument, from which an intent may be found that the sale could be made, would suffice as an element or factor from which to imply the power to sell. In regard to the property of the Church, as it has been said before, the vesting of a broad discretionary power in the trustee in matters pertaining to the trust, manifesting the intention to give to him quite general powers, may empower him to sell when circumstances indicate that the beneficiaries will experience difficulty in benefiting from the trust unless there is a sale.[24] It should be noted, however, that in the absence of any grant of authority to mortgage or pledge the property to meet certain contingencies, the

[23] *Ibid.*, § *162.*
[24] Cf. 40 *Ohio Jur.*, § *165.*

general rule is that there is no power to give mortgages upon such property or to pledge it.[25] It should also be emphasized that the trustee cannot encumber the *trust res* for his own benefit.[26] The power to mortgage may, however, be implied from the general tenor of the trust instrument when it is necessary from the point of view of the best interests of the beneficiary, or of the proper repair and care of the *trust res,* or when it is necessary to carry out the trust purpose. The court of equity, on application of the trustee, may, by virtue of its inherent jurisdiction over trusts, grant the permission to the trustee to mortgage the *trust res* as an incident to the general management of the trust when the best interests of the trust require it.[27]

Under ordinary circumstances, when it becomes desirable for one reason or another to sell or encumber land used for a place of worship, parsonage, or other religious purpose, a somewhat difficult question arises as to how the sale or encumbrance may be authorized, and who has power to convey the property. Quite generally it seems necessary to apply to some court for authority to sell property of such associations. The mere fact that the legal title to church property may be in its wardens, vestrymen, deacon, or other board as trustees, does not establish that they have a general right to convey such property. In Ohio, therefore, "when an established religious society desires to sell or encumber any real estate owned by it, or held in trust for a specified religious or charitable purpose, or held for its benefit by trustees, the officers entrusted with the management of its affairs, or holding title to such property, or, if incorporated, the society itself, may file in the common pleas court of the county where the land lies a petition

[25] Purcell *v.* Kuehn (1888), 5 Ohio Law Bulletin 442; The bishop, "being merely a trustee acting in a fiduciary capacity, cannot go beyond the power given to him in the deed of trust." (In this case there was no such authority found).

[26] Mannix *v.* Purcell, 46 Ohio State 102.

[27] *Page's Ohio General Code,* §§ 10,506-59 to 10,506-65.

stating how and by whom the land is held, (stating also) that a sale, lease, exchange, or encumbrance of the land is desired by the society, and that it is proper that such be done, and the court may authorize the prayer of the petition to be granted upon such terms as the court deems reasonable."[28] The petitioner must publish notice of the pendency and prayer of the petition in a newspaper of general circulation in the county once a week for four consecutive weeks.[29] Such a proceeding is not a civil action, but it is in the nature of a special proceeding, since it requires no summons to be issued.[30]

"When an application for the disposition of real property of a religious society is made to the court and the court authorizes a sale, lease, or encumbrance, the trustees or other officers of the society authorized to make the same must make return thereof to the court ordering it at such time as it orders. Thereupon the court, if satisfied that the sale, lease, exchange or encumbrance has been made according to its order, shall approve it and order that the proceeds be invested in other real estate for the use of the society, used in payment of its debts, or otherwise invested or disposed of according to the prayer of the petition."[31]

Article III. The Liability of Church Property

Property of a religious society is liable for its just debts as is that of an individual or civil corporation. The statutes of Ohio give effect to this principle by providing that, "when an incorporated religious congregation, society, association, sect or denomination uses or occupies as and for a place of worship, real estate which is held in trust for it or the members thereof, as and for a place of worship, and a judgment is recovered against such corporation, the

[28] *Page's Ohio General Code,* § 10,051.

[29] *Ibid.,* § 10,052.

[30] 35 *Ohio Jur.,* § 35.

[31] *Ibid.,* § 37.

real estate together with such edifice and improvements thereon, by a civil action for that purpose, shall be subjected to the payment of such judgment and costs."[32] "Real estate held in trust... for a place of worship or otherwise ... may be subjected to the payment of a judgment recovered against the trustees or committee..., in their individual capacity, or otherwise, for labor performed, materials furnished, or damages sustained, under any contract with them for the erection of a church edifice or other building or improvement made thereon."[33]

Religious corporations or associations are bound by, and are liable on, their contracts by the same principles of good faith and obligation which rest upon individuals and business corporations under like circumstances. An incorporated religious society is accountable for torts perpetrated by it. An action, however, for negligence cannot be maintained against the trustees of an unincorporated religious society in their representative capacity. In the case of such an organization, the members must be sued, for it cannot be sued in its own name. Under the doctrine, however, of parties by representation, a part of the members of an unincorporated religious society may sue or defend on behalf of all. This was done in the *Mannix v. Purcell* case, for although several congregations of churches, the land of which was held in trust by the Archbishop and the persons respectively possessing and having charge of such schools, cemeteries, and asylums, were severally unincorporated and otherwise incapable of holding the legal title to the property so used, they nevertheless had such an interest in the trust

[32] *Page's Ohio General Code,* § 10,002.

[33] *Ibid.,* § 10,014; In the *Mannix v. Purcell* case, however, it was stated that where property was held by the Archbishop in trust, to be devoted to the uses of public religious worship, cemeteries, orphan asylums, and schools, each church, cemetery, asylum and school is held upon a separate trust and for its own separate uses, and one piece of property so held is not chargeable with any part of the expense of improving another, nor of improving church property, generally, in the diocese. Cf. 46 Ohio State, 102.

property as permitted them to be represented in court by a number less than the whole, having a common interest with them for the purpose of protecting the property from seizure and sale for the satisfaction of the private debts of the trustee.[34]

[34] Cf. 35 *Ohio Jur.*, §§ 51-53.

CONCLUSIONS

The claim of the Church to sovereignty distinct from the State and its consistent efforts to exercise its property rights, independently of State authority, has been one of the factors causing many unfortunate disputes between the two sovereignties throughout the centuries. These disputes have often resulted in either a complete denial and disregard of the Church's native right to temporal goods, or the imposition of harmful restrictions upon the free exercise of that right in the achievement of the Church's divinely established end or purpose. (pp. 1-46)

In the United States, including the State of Ohio, the Church is not recognized as a juridically perfect or self-sufficient society, and its legal personality is denied. It cannot, therefore, acquire, hold and administer property independently of the civil authority, but it is permitted, within certain limitations, to exercise its rights indirectly. By respecting the rights of individual citizens to practice religion freely and to organize themselves into religious societies, the Government allows both citizens and societies to enjoy the benefits of property by holding it for the uses of charity and religion. (pp. 67-72)

In the state of Ohio the Church is permitted to hold property by two methods. It may resort to trust tenure, constituting, by deed, trustees who are permitted to acquire and hold property for its use and purpose; or it may incorporate by obtaining a charter of incorporation and thus it becomes an artificial person capable of acquiring and holding property subject to the provisions of the civil law. At the present time the greater part of church property belonging to the archdiocese and dioceses is held in trust by the respective ordinaries. The property of charitable and benevolent organizations operated by religious communities is held by the incorporated religious communities themselves. (pp. 72-81)

Property held by trust tenure is held passively and upon resulting trust, thereby granting to the bishop, as trustee, the right of wide discretionary management and control over the property. Ohio therefore recognizes those provisions of canon law which require this centralized control and power of disposal in the bishop, and which make the property available to the beneficiaries only for their use and enjoyment. Thus the bishop has a good measure of freedom in administering church property according to the provisions of canon law, for both Church and State demand that he keep it secure, make it productive, and apply it to the uses which are consistent with the purposes for which it is held. (pp. 81-86)

By recognizing the Church as a public charity the State of Ohio permits it to exercise its rights to donations and bequests of property, but not without restrictions. By an inheritance tax law Ohio taxes some of the Church's successions to property. It also imposes the burden of taxation upon that part of ecclesiastical property which it judges to be used not exclusively for purposes of divine worship. In doing so, it violates the Church's right to immunities which, by divine right, free all ecclesiastical possessions from tributes, assessments or payment of taxes imposed upon temporal goods by the civil law, and which, therefore, give to the Church the full and exclusive right over all of its property.

Ohio also violates the Church's right to succeed to gifts, devises, or bequests of property by invalidating those last wills and testaments which are not executed at least one year prior to the death of the testator. (pp. 86-96)

In applying its laws to church property, Ohio does not distinguish between that property which the Church sets apart by a consecration, by a blessing, or for some other reason, and which it states cannot be acquired by prescription or adverse possession, or cannot be given to profane uses. All such property is affected alike by the civil provisions. (pp. 67-96)

If, in the interest of holding and administering church property, it were considered desirable for the archdiocese and dioceses to incorporate, they could do so under the general incorporation law which, in Ohio, is quite liberally drafted. Within the framework of these incorporating statutes a diocesan and parochial corporation system could function for charitable and religious purposes with the necessary power of administration being vested in the bishop, as provided generally in the sacred canons. (pp. 67-127)

BIBLIOGRAPHY

Sources

Canon Law:

Acta et Decreta Concilii Plenarii Baltimorensis Tertii In Ecclesia Metropolitano Baltimorensi Habiti a die IX Novembris usque ad diem VII Decembris A.D. 1864, (Baltimorae: Typis Joannis Murphy et Soc.).

Acta Pii Papae IX ex quibus excerptus est Syllabus, Romae: Typis Rev. Camerae Apostolicae, 1865.

Codicis Iuris Canonici Fontes cura Emi Petri Card. Gasparri editi, 9 vols., Romae: Typis Polyglottis Vaticanis, 1923-1939. (Vols. VII-IX, ed. cura et studio Emi Iustiniani Card. Serédi).

Codex Iuris Canonici Pii X Pontificis Maximi iussu digestus, Benedicti Papae XV auctoritate promulgatus, Praefatione, Fontium Annotatione et Indice Analytico-Alphabetico ab Emo Petro Card. Gasparri Auctus, Romae, Typis Polyglottis Vaticanis, 1917; reimpressio, 1934.

Concilium Plenarium Totius Americae Septentrionalis Foederatae, Baltimori Tributum, (Baltimori: Apud Joannem Murphy et Socios, 1852, Decree n. 16.

Concilii Plenarii Baltimorensis II, In Ecclesia Metropolitana Baltimorensi Acta et Decreta, (Baltimorae: Joannes Murphy, 1868), Decrees nn. 182-188.

Decretales D. Gregorii Papae IX, suae integritati una cum glossis, restitutae, cum privilegio Gregorii XIII, Pont. Max., et Aliorum Principum, Romae, 1582.

Decretum Gratiani emendatum et notationibus illustratum cum glossis, Gregorii XIII, Pont. Max., iussu editum, 2 vols., Romae, 1582.

Denzinger, Heinrich-Bannwart, Clemens et Umberg, Johannes, *Enchiridion Symbolorum Definitionum et Declarationum de Rebus Fidei et Morum*, 21.-23. ed., St. Louis: Herder & Co., 1937.

Hardouin, Jean, *Acta Conciliorum et Epistolae Decretales ac Constitutiones Summorum Pontificum*, 12 vols., Parisiis, 1714-1715.

Liber Sextus Decretalium D. Bonifacii Papae VIII, suae integritati cum Clementinis et Extravagantibus, earumque Glossis restitutis, Romae, 1582.

Mansi, Joannes, *Sacrorum Conciliorum Nova et Amplissima Collectio*, 53 vols. in 60, Parisiis, 1901-1927.

Schroeder, H. J., *Canons and Decrees of the Council of Trent*, St. Louis: B. Herder Book Co., 1941.

Schroeder, H.J., *Disciplinary Decrees of the General Councils*, St. Louis: B. Herder Book Co., 1937.

Ohio Civil Law:

Ohio Jurisprudence: *A Complete Statement of the Law and Practice of the State of Ohio*, 43 vols., Vol. VIII, 1930; Vol. XII, 1936; Vol. XVI, 1938, (Cleveland: The Lawyers Cooperative Publishing Company).

Page, William H., *Page's Ohio General Code, Annotated*, Cincinnati: W. H. Anderson Company, 1938.

Page, William H., *Page's Ohio Revised Code, Annotated*, Cincinnati: W. H. Anderson Company, 1954.

Reference Works

Abbo, John A.-Hannan, Jerome D., *The Sacred Canons*, 2 vols., St. Louis: B. Herder Book Co., 1952.

Adams, George B.-Stephens, H. Morse, *Select Documents of English Constitutional History*, New York: The Macmillan Co., 1916.

Augustine, P. Chas., *A Commentary on the New Code of Canon Law*, 8 vols., Vol. VI, 2. ed., St. Louis: B. Herder Book Co., 1923.

Bartlett, Chester J., *The Tenure of Parochial Property in the United States of America*, The Catholic University of America Canon Law Studies, n. 31, Washington D.C.: The Catholic University of America, 1926.

Baronius, Ceasar, Card., *Annales Ecclesiastici*, 37 vols., Barri-Ducis, 1864-1883.

Blat, Albertus, *Commentarium Textus Codicis Iuris Canonici* 5 vols., Vol. II, Romae, 1919; Vol. III, Pars altera, Romae, 1923.

Bouvier, John, *Law Dictionary and Concise Encyclopedia*, 2 vols., Vol. I, 8. ed., St. Paul, Minn.: West Publishing Co., 1914.

Brown, Brendan F., *The Canonical Juristic Personality with Special Reference to its status in the United States of America*, The Catholic University of America Canon Law Studies, n. 39, Washington D.C.: The Catholic University of America, 1927.

Cappello, Felix, *Summa Iuris Canonici*, 3 vols., Vol. II, 4. ed., Romae: Apud Aedes Universitatis Gregorianae, 1945.

Catholic Encyclopedia, The, 15 vols., Index and Supplement, New York, 1907-1922.

Cocchi, Guidus, *Commentarium in Codicem Iuris Cannonici ad Usum Scholarum*, 8 vols., Vol. VI, 3. ed., Taurinorum Augustae: Marietti, 1933.

Creusen-Ellis-Garesché, *Religious Men and Women in the Code*, 4. ed., Milwaukee: Bruce Publishing Co., 1940.

DeMeester, Alphonsus, *Iuris Canonici et Iuris Canonico-Civilis Compendium*, nova ed., 3 vols., in 4, Brugis: Desclée, 1921-1928.

Dignan, Patrick J., *A History of the Legal Incorporation of Catholic Church Property in the United States*, New York: P. J. Kenedy & Sons, 1935.

Doheny, William J., *Church Property: Modes of Acquisition,* The Catholic University of America Canon Law Studies, n. 41, Washington D.C.: The Catholic University of America, 1927.

Evans, *A Collection of Statutes,* London. 1917.

Goodwine, John A., *The Right of the Church to Acquire Temporal Goods,* The Catholic University of America Canon Law Studies, n. 131, Washington D.C.: The Catholic University of America, 1941.

Guilday, Peter K., *A History of the Councils of Baltimore,* New York: The Macmillan Co., 1932.

Hannan, Jerome D., *The Canon Law of Wills,* The Catholic University of America Canon Law Studies, n. 86, Washington D.C.: The Catholic University of America, 1934.

Holdsworth, Sir William, *A History of English Law,* 13 vols., Vol. II, London: Methuen & Co. LTD., 1936.

Lamott, John H., *History of the Archdiocese of Cincinnati,* New York: Frederick Pustet Co., 1921.

Lecler, Joseph, *The Two Sovereignties:* A Study of the Relationship Between Church and State, New York: Philosophical Library Inc., 1952.

Lilly, William S.-Wallis, John E. P., *A Manual of the Law Specially Affecting Catholics,* London: William Clowes & Sons, 1893.

Martin, Thomas Owen, *Adverse Possession, Prescription and Limitation of Actions. The Canonical "Praescriptio,"* The Catholic University of America Canon Law Studies, n. 202, Washington D.C.: The Catholic University of America, 1944.

Ottaviani, Alaphridus, *Institutiones Iuris Publici Ecclesiastici,* 2 vols., Vol. I, 4. ed., Romae: Typis Polyglottis Vaticanis, 1947.

Pistocchi, M., *De Bonis Ecclesiae Temporalibus,* Taurini: Marietti, 1932.

Stephenson, Carl,-Marcham, Frederick G., *Sources of English Constitutional History,* New York: Harper & Brothers Publishers, 1937.

Stubbs, William, *The Constitutional History of England,* 3 vols., Vol. II, 3. ed., Oxford: The Clarendon Press, 1891.

Stubbs, William, *Select Charters of English Constitutional History,* 4. ed., London: The Clarendon Press, 1936.

Tanquerey, Ad., *Synopsis Theologiae Dogmaticae,* 3 vols., Vol. II, 24. ed., Parisiis; Desclée et Socii, 1937.

Thomassinus, L. *Vetus et Nova Ecclesiae Disciplina circa Beneficia et Beneficiarios,* 10 vols., Moguntini, 1786-1787.

Tosti, Luigi,-Donnelly, Eugene J., *History of Pope Boniface VIII and His Times, With Notes and Documentary Evidence,* 6 books in 1, New York: Christian Press Association, 1911.

Vermeersch, A.-Creusen, J., *Epitome Iuris Canonici,* 3 vols., Vol. II, 6. ed., Mechliniae-Romae: H. Dessain, 1940.

Vromant, G., *De Bonis Ecclesiae Temporalibus,* Louvain: Museum Lessianum, 1953.

Wernz, Franciscus Xaverius, *Ius Decretalium,* 6 vols., Romae, 1898-1914.

Wharton, J.J.S., *The Statute Law Now in Force Relating to Roman Catholics in England,* London: Spettigue and Farrance Co., 1851.

Woywod, Stanislaus, *A Practical Commentary on the Code of Canon Law,* revised by Callistus Smith, revised and enlarged edition, 2 vols., New York: Jos. F. Wagner, Inc., 1948.

Zollman, Carl, *American Church Law,* St. Paul, Minn.: West Publishing Co., 1933.

Zollman, Carl, *American Law of Charities,* Milwaukee: Bruce Publishing Co., 1924.

Ohio Cases Cited

American Bible Society *v.* Marshall, 15 Ohio State 537.

Andrews' Executors *v.* Andrews' Administrators, 7 Ohio State 143.

Berkemeyer *v.* Kellerman, 32 Ohio State 239.

Bloom *v.* Richards, 2 Ohio State 387.

Board of Education *v.* Minor, 23 Ohio State 211.

Broadrup *v.* Woodman, 27 Ohio State 553.

Cincinnati *v.* Cameron, 7 Am. L. Rec. 592.

Dayton *v.* Bartlett, 38 Ohio State 357.

Department of Taxation *v.* Forsythe, Executrix, 159 Ohio State 347.

Faurot *v.* Neff, 32 Ohio State 44.

First Presbyterian Society *v.* Langley, 25 Ohio State 128.

Gearhart *v.* Richardson, 109 Ohio State 418.

Gerke *v.* Purcell, 25 Ohio State 229.

Humphries *v* Little Sisters of the Poor, 29 Ohio State 201.

Kisor *v.* Stancifer, 6 Ohio State 363.

Manley *v.* Hunt, 1 Ohio Reports 257.

Mannix *v.* Purcell, 46 Ohio State, 102.

Mathews *v.* Leaman, 24 Ohio State 615.

McIntyre *v.* City of Zanesville, 17 Ohio State 352.

Miller *v.* Proctor, 20 Ohio State 442.

Miller *v.* Teachout, 24 Ohio State 525.

Minor *v.* Smith, 13 Ohio State 79.

Moeller *v.* Poland, 80 Ohio State 418.

Morgan *v.* Leslie, Wright (Ohio) 144.

Price et al. *v.* Methodist Church et al. 4 Ohio Reports 515.

Purcell *v.* Kuehn, 5 Ohio Law Bulletin 442.

Roche, Executor and Truste *v.* Department of Taxation, 138 Ohio State 145.

Salisbury *v.* Department of Taxation, 155 Ohio State 615.

Sowers *v.* Syremus, 39 Ohio State 29.
Trustees *v.* Zanesville Canal Co., 9 Ohio State 203.
Urmy *v.* Wooden, 1 Ohio State 160.
Watterson *v.* Halliday, 77 Ohio State, 150.
Watterson *v.* Ury, 5 Ohio Circuit Court 347.
Williams *v.* First Presbyterian Society, 1 Ohio State 478.
Willis *v.* Braucher, 79 Ohio State 290.
16 Wallace (U.S.) 36.

BIOGRAPHICAL NOTE

Urban C. Wiggins was born in Portsmouth, Ohio, January 14, 1921. He received his primary and preparatory education at Holy Redeemer Parochial School in that community. He entered Saint Charles Borromeo Seminary, Columbus, Ohio, in 1938, for his training in the classics and in philosophy. He was graduated from Saint Charles in 1942, receiving the degree of Bachelor of Arts. He completed his studies of the sacred sciences at Mount Saint Mary of the West Seminary, Norwood, Ohio, and was ordained a priest for the diocese of Columbus on October 27, 1945. On November 15, 1945, he was appointed to special work for the Diocesan Chancery Office. In 1946 he was made assistant pastor of Saint Joseph Cathedral, Columbus, Ohio, and during that appointment he served as Notary of the Diocesan Tribunal from 1949 to 1950. On June 15, 1950, he was appointed assistant pastor of Saint Mary Church, Marion, Ohio, and in October, 1952, he was admitted to the School of Canon Law of the Catholic University of America. He received the degree of the Baccalaureate in Canon Law in June, 1953, and the degree of the Licentiate in Canon Law in June, 1954.

ALPHABETICAL INDEX

www.ingramcontent.com/pod-product-compliance
Lightning Source LLC
LaVergne TN
LVHW050214080826
844660LV00012B/410